The Armageddon Spectre

D1572686

The Armageddon Spectre

HAROLD LINDSELL

CROSSWAY BOOKS • WESTCHESTER, ILLINOIS
A DIVISION OF GOOD NEWS PUBLISHERS

The Armageddon Spectre. Copyright © 1984 by Harold Lindsell. Published by Crossway Books, a division of Good News Publishers, Westchester, Illinois 60153.

Cover design by Lane T. Dennis

First printing, 1985

Printed in the United States of America

Library of Congress Catalog Card Number 84-72012

ISBN 0-89107-329-9

Contents

One: The Nuclear Threat   1

Two: God's Role   11

Three: Man's Role   20

Four: War in the Old Testament   27

Five: The View from the New Testament   38

Six: The Enemy   51

Seven: Communist Principles   62

Eight: Pacifism   74

Nine: Unilateral Disarmament   87

Ten: Nuclear Freeze   97

Eleven: Nuclear Deterrence   109

Twelve: Facing the Future   120

Notes   133

The Armageddon Spectre

1

The Nuclear Threat

Who can deny that a thermonuclear conflict is the most frightening menace today? The United States and the Soviet Union have atomic capability such as the world has never known; yet they do not have a monopoly on it. France, India, and Red China have nuclear bombs. With troops and nonnuclear weapons swarming the borders of Red China and Russia, nuclear confrontation between these powers is possible. We cannot be sure whether their apparent tensions are genuine, but neither can we rule out the possibility of collusion between these powers against the West.

Other nations have already produced or can produce instruments of destruction. Some of these smaller nations could detonate nuclear devices on a limited scale or even drop them on the major powers. Given the terrorism which exists today, the major powers do not constitute the only danger attached to the nuclear age.

If the Israelis were faced with another effort such as Hitler's to destroy them, they might resort to an atomic means to insure their survival.

Israel is surrounded by a vast throng of Arabs whose enmity for the Jews is openly stated and whose desire is that the state of Israel disappear from the face of the earth. The likelihood of any immediate change and the establishment of peaceful relations between Jew and Arab appears to be remote, but this should not discourage our peace efforts on behalf of them. Nations should work to prevent open conflict which could bring the Soviet Union and the United States into the situation. In a sense the two superpowers are hostage to decisions made by the Israelis. The United States, the one nation which has consistently supported Israel and has guaranteed its territorial integrity, despite some sharp differences, faces the greater danger.

It would be unfortunate not to recognize that the Arab peoples think they have a just cause for opposing Israel. Nor should Christians who believe that the return of the Jews to Palestine is part of God's plan of the ages be insensitive to the plight of the Arabs who have been forcibly removed from homes and villages they have occupied for hundreds of years. We do not know how it would have been possible for the Jews to come back to what they have considered to be their homeland and at the same time to have made provisions for those who were forced to leave.

The Arab world itself is not a single entity, and the various segments cannot agree. Arab nations also may have the capacity to manufacture and detonate atom bombs. Given the hostility between the Arabs and the Israelis, it is possible that an Arab nation might use nuclear threat for blackmail or actually to drop a bomb on Israel or on other nations.

Potential Consequences

Today more people are aware of the potential consequences of nuclear war than ever before. Especially among the nations of the West, people recognize the awful devastation and loss of life that would result from nuclear war. They understand that these results would effect participants and nonparticipants alike, and that even neighboring nations not directly involved in such a war could suffer. The possibility of extinction is cited, in a grim picture of The Silent Planet. Even though people distinguish between the possibility of extinction and the reality of it, it is the *possibility* which drives many to activities to prevent nuclear war by eliminating all such weaponry.

Ideally no one in his right mind and good heart would

object to eliminating all nuclear weapons. Nor would any such person oppose worldwide disarmament and the solving of national and international problems by arbitration and other peaceful means. But reason informs us that all life on the planet could also be destroyed by other less threatening means than nuclear bombs. Weapons of the nonnuclear type which nations now possess are a danger. In World War II Europe was devastated by explosives dropped from ever-increasing numbers of bombers stationed in Britain, not to mention the damage inflicted on that nation by Nazi attacks. The nonnuclear capacity of the nations to wreak the severest damage by conventional means is far greater than it was during World War II, and this ability is increasing.

Chemical warfare further enhances the danger of annihilation. Some of the deadliest microorganisms known to man are in national arsenals. These are so lethal that were they to contaminate water supplies, the death toll would be comparable to that brought about by nuclear bombs. The "yellow rain" in the Far East has decimated populations. Reports of death by chemical warfare in Afghanistan can be dismissed only by overlooking or discounting the data compiled against the Soviet military by expert and trustworthy sources. Any success in eliminating nuclear weaponry would still leave our planet open to destruction by chemical means.

Frightening as nuclear and chemical weaponry are, no one can dismiss the dismal probability of a death ray weapon. Laser technology is advancing so rapidly that by 1990 the Soviet Union may have what some have called the ultimate weapon for use against the West. Robert Moss, in his novel *Death Beam,* has advanced a chilling scenario, but Major General George J. Keenan, Jr., former chief of the U.S. Air Force Intelligence, points to its possible reality: "Just as Churchill warned of the rise of Nazi Germany on the eve of World War II, Moss has charted the next road to Armageddon." Allen Drury, author of *Advise and Consent,* in the preface to *Death Beam* underscores the reality: "Moss reveals again his intimate knowledge of the activities of the KGB and its Western counterparts . . . and fashions a vivid story of what may lie just ahead when the laser beam moves out of the realm of science fiction and becomes a reality."

Allan C. Brownfeld, in a review of *Death Beam* in the March 1983 issue of *America's Future,* concluded:

> Unfortunately, there is more truth than fiction in this important book. The CIA has, indeed, underestimated Soviet defense spending—and accomplishments—for many years. The CIA told us that Moscow was not developing a massive defense program—just as the program was rapidly proceeding. Even now, in 1983, the CIA is trying to convince the world that Moscow and its satellites had no role in the attempted assassination of the Pope. Those who read *Death Beam* may be able to make sense of our increasingly unreal reality.

The threat the world faces from conventional arms, chemical warfare, nuclear bombs, and laser technology is alarming. It is possible for men of science to create a situation on this planet which life cannot endure. It is theoretically possible to pollute the atmosphere to such a degree that genetic changes might imperil the future of the human race. It is even possible that all life might be extinguished. As these threats permeate our consciousness we need to evaluate our options.

One Man's Response
Professor Gordon D. Kaufman of Harvard Divinity School delivered the presidential address before the members of the American Academy of Religion in December of 1982. His subject was "Nuclear Eschatology and the Study of Religion." He painted the worst feasible picture of what nuclear holocaust might be like:

> In three articles in the *New Yorker* last February [1982], subsequently published in the widely discussed book, *The Fate of the Earth,* Jonathan Schell presents a meditation on nuclear warfare. Schell's descriptions of the effects of such a

war on human beings are as horrifying in every detail as one might expect. But he goes beyond simply cataloging the almost unimaginable suffering such a conflict would bring, to point out that it might well signal the extinction of the human race. Indeed, the poisoning and radical transformation of the earth's upper atmosphere could make impossible the survival of many forms of life, thus returning our planet to its original largely barren and dead condition—except for one important difference: the atmosphere in those primordial ages here on earth was conducive to the evolution of countless species of life; the atmosphere after a nuclear holocaust would be irredeemably poisoned for a very long future.

The burden of Schell's articles, however, is not simply to set before us those facts—or possible facts—as information which all up-to-date men and women should have at their fingertips. It is, rather, to meditate for us and with us on what these facts mean, to call to our attention, in a way that has not, perhaps, been done before, the utterly new historical situation into which the possibility of all-out nuclear warfare has brought humanity.[1]

Dr. Kaufman was so moved by what he had learned that he concluded: "We may be about to annihilate the whole human future, and we must take the responsibility for that fact. We must try to understand it, and we must seek for symbols to interpret it." Certainly no one can afford to take a position of disinterested aloofness from the nuclear question. It requires a response.

Professor Kaufman was deeply exercised by the philosophic question raised by Jonathan Schell, who is not a theologian, nor does he seem to have a particular bent toward the religious. Dr. Kaufman quotes him as follows:

The possibility that the living can stop the future generations from entering into life compels us to ask basic new questions about our existence, the most sweeping of which is what these unborn ones . . . mean to us. No one has ever thought to ask this question before our time, because no generation before ours has ever held the life and death of the species in

its hands. . . . how are we to comprehend the life or death of
the infinite number of possible people who do not yet exist
at all? How are we, who are a part of human life, to step
back from life and see it whole, in order to assess the meaning of its disappearance? . . . Death cuts off life; extinction
cuts off birth. Death dispatches into the nothingness after
life each person who has been born; extinction in one stroke
locks up in the nothingness before life all the people who
have not yet been born. . . . The threat of the loss of birth
. . . assails everything that people hold in common, for it is
the ability of our species to produce new generations which
assures the continuation of the world in which all of our
common enterprises occur and have their meaning.[2]

Another Annihilation

It seems to have escaped both Jonathan Schell and Gordon
Kaufman that the ultimate annihilation of all life about which
they speak is already taking place in a smaller context through
abortion. One might well ask the difference between cutting off
birth by abortion for the few and cutting off birth for many by
extinction. Since in Schell's view death ends all, what ultimate
difference does it make to him if all life ceases on this planet
earth? One also might ask, if it is not immoral to abort fetuses,
why would it be immoral to destroy all life? We should note
that through the ages Christianity has stood firmly against
abortion. Surely we must address the nuclear question too.

Dr. Kaufman differs from Jonathan Schell in that he professes to move within the Christian tradition and allows for the
existence of God. He is well aware of traditional theology when
he asserts:

The religious eschatology of the West was undergirded by
faith in an active creator and governor of history, one who
from the beginning was working out purposes which were
certain to be realized as history moved to its consummation.
The end of history, thus—whether viewed as ultimate catastrophe or ultimate salvation—was to be God's climactic act.
The consummation was something that the faithful could

live with—even look forward to with hope—for it would be the moment when God's final triumph over all evil powers was accomplished.[3]

Dr. Kaufman properly states that in Christian theology "mankind was never believed to have the power utterly to destroy itself; that power lay with God alone." He goes on to say:

> If we wish to interpret our catastrophic event in terms of these traditions (i.e., that Christian tradition), two alternatives appear to be open to us. Either we can assert that the ultimate catastrophe, if it comes, is in some sense God's will and God's doing, that the annihilation of humanity which God had contemplated during the time of Noah is now coming to pass through a nuclear holocaust instead of a flood. Or we may hold that God, as the redeemer and savior of mankind as well as our creator, has so bound Godself (sic) to humanity and the human enterprise . . . that this utterly calamitous self-destruction of humanity will never be allowed to occur.
>
> Each of these alternatives affirms the ultimate sovereignty of God over the events of history—an indispensable point for biblical faith. . . . But clearly neither of these interpretations grants what is central and novel in this potential event as it confronts our consciousness today, namely, that it will be we human beings who are absolutely responsible if this catastrophe occurs. That this event confronts us as an act of human doing, not of divine will. . . .
>
> Some fundamentalists on the far religious right, following out the implications of the biblical apocalyptic imagery of an earthly holocaust as the ultimate expression of God's sovereignty over history, are apparently willing to go so far as to suggest that a nuclear disaster, if it ever comes, could only be an expression of the purpose of God; hence, any who work to prevent such a climax to human history are in fact guilty of opposing God's will (see *Boston Globe*, 5/2/82, p. A-1).

Along with such convictions, as one might expect, goes the demand that America arm itself to the teeth in the preparation for the coming Armageddon. But surely to take such a position is not only an ultimate evasion of our responsibility as human beings, it is demonically to invoke the divine will as a justification for that very evasion.[4]

Man's Responsibility?

Professor Kaufman goes on to state clearly that the God known by men in earlier times and as revealed in the Bible is finite and thus limited in his power. He argues that "the personalistic conception of God, so powerfully presented by the traditional images of Christian and Jewish piety, seems less and less defensible in face of the issues humanity today confronts," and that the present situation calls for a theology which forces on us "changes in our religious symbolism and in the frames of reference within which we make our value judgments and moral choices." He is saying that since God is impotent, man must assume the burden alone. He continued:

> Instead of assuming that we already know from revelation or authoritative tradition the correct values and standards—the faith orientation—in terms of which life is to be understood, and decisions and actions formulated, we must recognize and acknowledge that humankind has moved into a historical situation unanticipated by biblical writers and subsequent theological commentators alike, a situation of much greater knowledge, power and responsibility than our religious traditions have ever imagined possible.[5]

Given Professor Kaufman's presupposition that God is not able to handle the present crisis, he is forced to rest his confidence in man. This is an approach consistent with the thinking Western culture inherited from the Enlightenment, thinking that elevated human reason above revelation. Human reason determines what man shall believe and do. We must make a choice between reason freed from revelation or revelation in which reason is subordinate to it.

It was not unnatural for Dr. Kaufman to find the only hope for man's deliverance among the religious intelligentsia with whom he has worked for years. His final plea is to harness the resources of these learned men and women to attack the nuclear threat and bring peace to the earth before all life is extinguished. He says:

> Collectively, we in the American Academy of Religion have at our fingertips a greater knowledge of the religious resources of humankind—the resources, that is to say, for grappling with the problems of mystery and finitude—than any other group on this continent, possibly in the world. We have done virtually nothing to bring that knowledge and those resources to bear on the present crisis. Can we really continue, in the name of "neutrality" and "objectivity," to pursue our academic work in this kind of aloofness from the potential disaster that confronts humanity?[6]

The Options

This Harvard Divinity School professor has laid before us the options. We can choose his option in which man accepts full responsibility for the current crisis and works out his own solution to prevent the annihilation of life on this planet, or we can stand firm in the tradition of theological orthodoxy and believe that God neither sleeps nor rests.

Dr. Kaufman's suggested program includes (1) stopping the arms race and looking to the eventual elimination of all nuclear weaponry; (2) breaking the back of the nation-states system, which means one world government; (3) reorienting the priorities of consumption and distribution of the world's goods, which again means some form of international control or socialism; (4) finding a way to live with one another productively and justly on this earth and without warfare. Though idealism is to be commended, the absence of specifics dims the vision. The failure to consider the nature of man or to suggest how the new man can be brought into being leaves an enormous gap between the ideal and its attainment. He suggests no determinative role for God, although it is apparent that the academicians he addresses are to grapple with that question and discover what role there is for God, if any.

Those who choose the second option—acknowledging God has a role—must make a further decision regarding the extent of his participation. Here there are three choices. One is that God started the universe, established its laws, and left it to itself or to man, as the deists allege. Another suggests God is finite and, while operative in the affairs of men, cannot determine ends, for he is not wholly sovereign or omnipotent. The third choice is that God is sovereign, omnipotent, omniscient, omnipresent, and in charge of all things—the view of the churches for millennia. The latter view is affirmed in Scripture. It is this one that we will develop, looking at its implications in connection with the nuclear menace.

Along with this we must also consider what we should do about the problem, if anything, under the sovereignty of God. Historical orthodoxy generally has not said that man is a puppet who responds when the strings are pulled and is cast hither and yon by an invisible hand.

As we turn our attention to God's role from creation to consummation, we will be in a better position to consider what we can do to prevent the use of nuclear bombs by the United States or by any other nation.

2

God's Role

Christian orthodoxy starts with the presupposition that God is, and that he has spoken. He has spoken through nature, which testifies to his creativity and existence. But man cannot know God through nature. God must be self-revealing for us to know him. The revelation of God himself comes to us through the written Word—the Bible—and through the Word of God incarnate—the Lord Jesus Christ. Since the only Jesus we know is the Jesus of the Bible, the Bible and Jesus Christ stand or fall together. We cannot separate one from the other without the loss of both. God has spoken through the Bible, declaring his nature and his sovereignty. He existed before the world and is independent of it. To him nothing can be added or taken away. He is the God of knowledge, holiness, and power. He is infinite in his being and perfections.

Whatever we say about the nuclear threat must be derived immediately or derivatively from the revelation of God. Derivative judgments must not contradict the Bible, which is the source of our religious knowledge both as it relates to the past and to the future. From it we know that God is present and at work in our universe.

God's Sovereignty
The Bible teaches that God is in charge of men and nations, and what they do is determined at last by his will and design. It also illustrates what God has done in the history of man and

affirms his sovereignty. Sovereignty by its very meaning allows that God is supreme in power. What he decides must take place. No man or nation can prevent what he wills from occurring.

When God appeared and spoke to Abraham he said: "I am Almighty God" (Genesis 17:1). The prophet Jeremiah understood God's power. He said: "Ah, Lord God! Behold, you have made the heavens and the earth by your great power and outstretched arm. There is nothing too hard for you" (Jeremiah 32:17). The Psalmist proclaimed: "But our God is in heaven; he does whatever he pleases" (115:3). And again: "Whatever the Lord pleases he does, in heaven and in earth, in the seas and in all deep places" (Psalm 135:6). Jesus, the Word of God incarnate, endorsed the omnipotence of God when he said, "With God all things are possible" (Matthew 19:26).

The Bible asserts that King Cyrus was used by God to accomplish his purposes. Cyrus "is my shepherd, and he shall perform all my pleasure. . . . Thus says the Lord to his anointed, to Cyrus, whose right hand I have held—to subdue nations before him and loose the armor of kings, to open before him the double doors, so that the gates will not be shut" (Isaiah 44:28; 45:1).

Nebuchadnezzar's life affords us a series of illustrations about God's sovereignty over the nations. Jeremiah declared that Nebuchadnezzar was God's instrument to punish Jerusalem. He said that God said:

> I myself will fight against you [that is, against Zedekiah and Jerusalem] with an outstretched hand and with a strong arm, even in anger and fury and great wrath. I will strike the inhabitants of this city, both man and beast; they shall die of a great pestilence. And afterward, says the Lord, I will deliver Zedekiah king of Judah, his servants and his people, and such as are left in this city from the pestilence and the sword and the famine, into the hand of Nebuchadnezzar king of Babylon, into the hand of their enemies, and into the hand of those who seek their life; and he shall strike them with the edge of the sword. He shall not spare them, or have pity or mercy. (Jeremiah 21:5-7)

Daniel illustrates the sovereign, omnipotent power of God in the life of Nebuchadnezzar in two instances. One occurred in connection with Nebuchadnezzar's dream of the four kingdoms. Daniel spoke the word of God to the king: "You, O king, are a king of kings. For the God of heaven has given you a kingdom, power, strength, and glory; and wherever the children of men dwell, or the beasts of the field and the birds of the heaven, he has given them into your hand, and has made you ruler over them all" (Daniel 2:37, 38).

Later God punished Nebuchadnezzar for his consuming pride. A voice from heaven said to him: "King Nebuchadnezzar, to you it is spoken: the kingdom has departed from you! And they shall drive you from men, and your dwelling shall be with the beasts of the field. They shall make you eat grass like oxen; and seven times shall pass over you, until you know that the Most High rules in the kingdom of men, and gives it to whomever he chooses" (Daniel 4:31, 32).

The Psalmist wrote: "For exaltation comes neither from the east nor from the west nor from the south. But God is the Judge: he puts down one and exalts another" (75:6). When Moses wrote Deuteronomy, he recorded the word of God's future judgment against his people Israel, whom he knew would become apostate. He said: "The Lord will scatter you among all peoples, from one end of the earth to the other, and there you shall serve other gods, which neither you nor your fathers have known—wood and stone. And among those nations you shall find no rest, nor shall the sole of your foot have a resting place; but there the Lord will give you a trembling heart, failing eyes, and anguish of soul" (Deuteronomy 28:64, 65).

The Book of Amos is filled with evidences of God's immediate control over the nations of the earth. Judgment is pronounced against Damascus, Gaza, Edom, Ammon, and Moab, as well as Samaria and Judah. All of this took place. Micah repeated the pronouncement of God's judgment on Israel and Judah.

Just as God determines what will happen to nations, so he also executes judgment on individuals. In the New Testament we read of Herod's persecution of the church. The king reached a place where he was being deified by the people. As they shouted that his was "the voice of a god and not of a man" (Acts 12:22), the sovereign judgment of God fell on him: "Immediately an angel of the Lord struck him, because he did not give glory to God. And he was eaten by worms and died" (12:23).

In addition to specific statements about the divine presence in the affairs of men and nations, we read in the Bible general statements which reinforce the truth that God has his hands over the affairs of this earth. "The Lord of hosts has sworn, saying, 'Surely, as I have thought, so shall it come to pass, and as I have purposed, so it shall stand' " (Isaiah 14:24). Later, through Isaiah, God spoke: "My counsel shall stand, and I will do all my pleasure" (Isaiah 46:10). The Psalmist wrote: "The counsel of the Lord stands forever, the plans of his heart to all generations" (33:11).

God's Foreknowledge
Any consideration of the sovereignty of God must take into account his foreknowledge as well. God knows the end from the beginning. There is nothing he does not know. Nothing can take him by surprise. The acts of men or of nations in the past, now, or in the future were known by God in eternity past.

God also knows all the possibilities. To liken the operations of God among men to that of a game of chess, we could say that if God were to play a thousand games at the same time he would know all of the possible moves and what each move involves, down to the last one when he checkmates the opponent.

At all times God knows how many fish are in the waters of the world, how many stars in the galaxies, and how many grains of sand on the seashores. Anything less would mean that God is not truly God. He would be finite.

From a philosophical perspective we might ask, if God foreknows all things, must they occur because he foreknows them? Whatever he foreknows must take place. If he foreknows only contingently, so that something could come up to annul what he foreknew, then foreknowledge would partake of finitude and God would no longer be God. How can it be otherwise, once we accept the concept of omniscience?

Some might ask further, does God look down the pathways of the future to discern how men will act so that his foreknowledge is contingent on what men will do? Are his plans and his decisions made *after* the fact or before the fact? This question is related to foreordination as well. Theologians have wrestled with the problem of the relationship of foreknowledge to foreordination. Opinions differ, for finite man is faced with divine mysteries at many levels and does not have final answers to some questions this side of eternity. In any event, we do know from the Bible that God accomplishes his purposes. No one can defeat his pleasure or his purposes.

Is it not biblically and logically conceivable that God should have to change his plans, annul his purpose, or enjoy a foreknowledge that is relative rather than absolute? No. The One who created all things by the word of his power also preserves his creation by that same power, and controls creation so that nothing can abridge or alter his plans. This has implications for present-day problems and particularly for the prophetic or eschatological Word of God with regard to the end of history or the consummation.

God's Absolutes
The Bible reveals that life on planet earth will not continue forever. History as we know it will end. The end is related to the final judgment and is based upon the assertion that a payday is coming. All the ethnic religions agree that sin, however badly it is defined, exists in the world, and that fact supposes that there is something which is right, eternal, and retributive. If there is only evil and no good, there is nothing to talk about. The eschatological dimension is based upon good and evil, upon the notion of a warfare between God and Satan, between right and wrong. The nature of the universe is such that wrong must perish and right prevail.

We live in a moral universe and all men, even the Marxists, have some view of right and wrong. If there is no God, from whence have men come to recognize the distinction between good and evil, between love and hate, between life and death? Indeed, if there is no God, how can there be a moral universe unless this is the invention of the human mind? Since mankind differs widely in ideas and perceptions, how could anything moral, loving, or good prevail unless it is at least utilitarian? Without absolutes, there is no way by which love can be shown to be better than hate or morality better than immorality. And if morality, love, and good are to be found innately in the universe without God, there can be no mind from which it springs, and man becomes a mere instrument of a mechanistic world which robs him of his dignity and makes him a creature of nonbeing.

The Bible straightforwardly proclaims that moral absolutes come from God, that man is living in a period of probation, and that God has appointed a day of judgment. That day is set in the mind of God. Just as the incarnation of Jesus took place precisely in accord with the plan of God, so will the consummation. The day and the hour are hidden in the counsels of God until manifested in history for all to see. The key to the consummation is Jesus Christ who, according to the Bible, is coming again. This Second Advent will mark the end of history as we know it. Evil will be dealt with at last, and righteousness and the utopia for which the hearts of good men yearn will prevail forever. Between the ascension of Jesus to heaven and his return from heaven to earth is a period marked by wars and rumors of wars. Men of evil bent will do terrible things, filling hearts with fear. Evil will increase. Tumults will come upon the earth, and even the heavens will be shaken. All of this is part of God's plan leading to the consummation. Men will have their final opportunity to turn from their wickedness to Jesus Christ and to righteousness.

Nuclear energy is not new to God, nor does the threat of nuclear holocuast take him by surprise. Whether we conclude that the nuclear problem comes from the permissive or the directive will of God makes no essential difference, but as it *is* new to man its coming has created a situation far graver than anything man has encountered in his history. People are frightened and rightly imagine an atomic war wiping out this planet.

But they can reach this conclusion only from the human perspective, failing to allow for God in the total picture. In all that we see and face in this generation God is speaking to us about his divine intention. We do not know, however, whether the consummation is at hand or will come about a thousand or 10,000 years from now.

Annihilation?

The Bible clearly states that Jesus Christ is coming again to draw his own to himself. When he comes, millions or billions of people will still be on this planet. He will not return to a silent planet with no life and no people. Were this to happen, it would represent a victory of evil over good, of Satan over God. Annihilation of all life is a threat which cannot become a reality. God is in charge and will not permit annihilation to take place.

If God is not able to prevent annihilation, should we not understand that the likelihood of man preventing what God cannot prevent is minuscule? Given the nature of man, annihilation would surely come about. The planet would no longer hear the sounds of children at play or men at work or women giving birth to future generations. The prospects would be dismal indeed.

Men of goodwill need not lose heart. God surely will muzzle and control those who might be willing to exterminate all life whether by intention or by accident. This can be affirmed only because God is both transcendent and imminent. He is above and within. He is there, and he is also here. He has not and will not abdicate his throne.

Christians and the Consummation

The fact that this planet will not be destroyed by nuclear holocaust does not mean that nuclear weaponry will not be used. Even limited use of such armaments would be highly destructive; therefore reasonable men, including Christians, should try to prevent any use of nuclear bombs. If there are, in fact, Christians who say that to prevent a nuclear climax opposes God's will, they should reexamine their conclusions, for they are on shaky ground. It is important to make clear that such people constitute a small minority.

In the first place the Bible nowhere suggests that God is going to end history by wiping out all life on the planet earth. In 2 Peter we read that there will come a time when "the heavens will pass away with a great noise, and the elements will melt with fervent heat; both the earth and the works that are in it will be burned up" (3:10). This Scripture does not refer to an event which will occur before the Second Advent of Jesus Christ. It refers to a time after the consummation when the earth will be renovated and the stains of sin removed. For the millennialists, this event will occur *after* the thousand-year rule of Christ on earth. For the nonmillennialists, this event will occur shortly after the coming of Jesus Christ and subsequent to the final judgment. In either case, no people will be on the earth when this takes place; all will have been judged and assigned either to life in the presence of God or eternal death outside the divine presence. Then the purgation will come.

Any enterprising reporter can find a few people who make rash and unsupported observations based on either a misunderstanding of the Bible or a lack of biblical knowledge. On the whole, the religious right has a better track record *vis-a-vis* the consummation of history than do the secular humanists or even theological liberals who veer away from biblical revelation and support reason above revelation.

It is fair to say that some fundamentalists and/or evangelicals show no disposition to get involved in the efforts to prevent nuclear war, but there are many unbelievers who have no interest in the subject either. Wholly apart from religious convictions, people are people and never has there been complete consensus on any question. If we count the numbers of those who march against and protest nuclear bombs, it is clear that those who do not march and do not register protests number the vast majority of the world's population.

Moreover, the very thought of nuclear holocaust is so frightening that many shrink from thinking about it and pretend the problem doesn't exist. A head-in-the-sand attitude by anyone is hardly commendable, but these people probably sleep better than do those who are aware of the problem and involved in seeking a solution. Christians, however, should face the nuclear question head-on and express their views publicly. The Christian faith commands that we should love God and neighbors, and pray for our enemies. We must do this in the light of the fact that "when we were enemies we were reconciled to God" (Romans 5:10). Moreover, Christians are encouraged to help the poor and feed the hungry. Surely if this is true, then saving the lives of people by preventing the detonation of nuclear devices would follow. The preservation of life is so significant to fundamentalists and evangelicals that they are among the most active in opposing abortion-on-demand. If this is so, to fail to be concerned about nuclear warfare would be inconsistent. More baffling is that many activists who are hard at work to prevent nuclear catastrophe are among the most fervent supporters of abortion-on-demand. On principle, Christians should work to eliminate nuclear bombs, chemical weaponry, tanks and conventional weapons, future laser weapons, and wars of any kind anywhere around the globe. Whether such efforts succeed or whether international problems can be resolved by arbitration and goodwill are open questions. The fact that the Bible prophesies wars and rumors of wars does not mean that Christians should not seek the end of wars. Wars are fought because men are wicked. They are evil, and the consequences are destructive. Given the world situation, we are called upon to make clear what the Bible teaches about these matters, but we do so with the certain knowledge that God is sovereign, that wicked men can go so far and no further, and that even the worst of evil men will be prevented by God from destroying all life on the planet earth. God has revealed this to be so in the Bible, and he has the power and the will to insure that total nuclear destruction will not happen.

3

Man's Role

In assessing the role of man in the nuclear dilemma, we must understand the nature of man. Christian theology teaches that God made man and woman in the moral and spiritual image of their Creator. Adam and Eve became the progenitors of the entire human race. They walked in fellowship with God and were perfect, but they were not omniscient.

Adam was given full control over the Garden of Eden in which he and Eve were placed and told not to eat the fruit of the tree of the knowledge of good and evil. God warned Adam that if he ate of the fruit of that tree he would die, would be separated from God. Eve ate of the fruit first. When she urged her husband to eat of the fruit, he did so and brought to their descendants the consequences of his transgression.

Saved and Lost

Since Adam's fall, all human beings have been born as sinners. But God provided a way for all to be forgiven and made right with him. He sent his son Jesus Christ to take the punishment for man's sin by dying on the cross. Those who trust in him and acknowledge his death for their sin are saved. Those who do not are lost. Important changes take place in the saved. They become new creations in Christ Jesus (2 Corinthians 5:17). They are "renewed in the knowledge of their Creator" (Colossians 3:10).

Marxists acknowledge that there is something fundamentally wrong with man and they want to change him too, but the "new creation" they desire is a proletarian who thinks according to Marxist ideology and who will remake the world according to the tenets of Marxism. They envision that Communists will constitute a perfect classless society which will function when all who are not in accord with this vision are eliminated. In their minds this must take place in the here and now, for there is no future for man after death. The Marxists' "new man" is a faith-promise based on imagination, whereas the Christian new man has the promise of immortality based on the historical account of Christ's resurrection, a fact corroborated by the testimony of many witnesses.

Whereas formerly it was impossible to think in a Christ-like way, the new man in Christ can do precisely that, although he does not always do so. The unbeliever, however, cannot think like Christ because his mind is still darkened by sin. Thus when we appraise views on nuclear warfare, it is necessary to consider the source and perspective of those views. The unbelieving mind, whether Marxist or of some other bent, and the believing mind are antithetical. For a Christian to do business with a Marxist, for example, believing that the Marxist mind thinks similarly, is like committing suicide.

The Role of Law
All nations and all men are governed by some rule of law, whether written or unwritten. No society, large or small, can continue to function without rules. Even savages in the jungle have rules which bind them together, though they vary widely from those of advanced cultures. Societies without the benefit of biblical revelation and without the knowledge of the true God still have the light of nature; and however marred and defaced by sin, human conscience knows something about right and wrong. If people cannot trust each other, they have no way by which a viable relationship can be established and maintained. If trust does not exist, suspicion eats as a cancer, and life knows no security or peace. The question of relationship begins with the family, which is a microcosm that mirrors a nation-state. A man and a woman in marriage will not continue in fellowship without trust.

In a perfect society there would be no need for law, because all people would do what they should. But once a situation exists in which people do what they should not do, law becomes necessary. If no one ever steals, there is no need for a law against stealing. If everyone always tells the truth, there is no need to forbid lying. Law is based upon the fact that men are sinners and need to be restrained; yet restraints have little meaning if they are not accompanied by penalties against those who violate the law.

Unregenerate man is characterized by the will to do what he should not. He thinks himself to be autonomous, freed from God and his law. This is the kind of man who lies, cheats, and steals, who begins wars, oppresses the innocent, and steals bread from the orphans and the poor. What is true of individuals is also true of nations. Nations do not make decisions; men do. The decision-makers are either good or bad; they are either believers in the laws of equity and justice, or they are not.

In the Western world Hugo Grotius set forth four basic principles which were to govern the relationships between humans, and between states:

(1) No state or individual may attack another state or individual.

(2) No state or individual may appropriate what belongs to another state or individual.

(3) No state or individual may disregard treaties or contracts.

(4) No state or individual may commit a crime.

Grotius was a theologian as well as a legal expert. Undoubtedly the principles he articulated were grounded in a commitment to biblical Christianity and God's absolutes. His views rose out of the idea of a moral universe with God, the Lawgiver, revealing principles which would allow men and nations to live in harmony. We might suppose that the same or similar principles could flow from human reason and be based on a utilitarian view of life. And surely thoughtful men would agree that the use of such principles would be favorable to all.

Yet, Grotius' principles, good as they are and even though they may be derived from the Bible, are workable only if men and nations accept and support them. In general, individuals and nations have never done this, because they are imperfect and put their interests ahead of these principles. They abide by them when it is beneficial to do so, but when it hurts or hinders them, they flagrantly violate these principles. In most cases self-interest takes precedence over the interest of others. Moreover, the accidents of life and history produce circumstances in which the principles by their very nature cannot work equitably. Small nations are disadvantaged when their interests conflict with those of neighboring nations larger in size, population, and power.

Poland is a classical case of being surrounded by two large and powerful countries, the Soviet Union and Germany. The problem rises from the geography of Europe. It makes little difference whether the Soviet Union is ruled by czars or the Communists, or whether Germany is ruled by Nazis or a monarch. Poland has been caught in a nutcracker. Its long history has been marked by invasions from the east and the west, and by the partition of the nation again and again among the greater powers. If all nations were peaceful and exhibited brotherly love, there would be no problem; but nothing leads us to believe that they will act differently.

Why the Law Is Broken
When nations break the law, they offer explanations and excuses to justify their actions. Usually they cite the need to protect the national interest. The nation that starts a war ostensibly believes that the nation against which it commits aggression presents a danger to it. In the case of Adolph Hitler, the Soviet Union presented a danger. To attack the Soviet Union, it was necessary to get there through Poland. Poland represented no genuine threat to Germany, but Russia did. The Soviet Union believes that the occupation of the Baltic states, the neutralization of Finland, and the control of Poland is essential to its own territorial safety. The same reasoning underlies Soviet aggression against Czechoslovakia, Hungary, and Romania.

The Soviets want a shield against the West, which means that any attack on the Soviet Union from the ground must first pass through the shield these nations provide.

When one nation commits an act of aggression against another nation, the law of nations has been violated. Do the uninvolved countries who are in agreement with the law of nations have an obligation to defend the invaded nation? This question was posed by Zbigniew Brzezinski on a television interview when he asked: "What are the moral implications of passivity?" He was not talking about pacifism. He was talking about the moral implications of doing nothing when the occasion calls for response.

When naked aggression takes place, few if any nations who have no self-interest in the matter will employ force against an aggressor. The Soviet invasion of Afghanistan brought about no military response by the nations of the world. Those whose interests are not at stake could hardly care less. Moreover, most of the nations are in no position to do anything that would cripple the invader. Those who could do something don't. The United States has not responded with force to evict the Soviets from Afghanistan, nor does it appear that the American people would support such a response. The rule of law over the nations is limited if for no other reason than that it can be broken with impunity. The only way by which the invasion of Afghanistan could have been averted would have been the knowledge that the nations of the world in concert and by the use of force would have intervened to preserve the territoriality of Afghanistan. Since the Soviets knew that the nations would do nothing to support the people of Afghanistan, Russia confidently went ahead with the invasion.

Force Requires Force

When a nation employs armed force, the only adequate response is the use of force as a countervailent. War is required to counter war. This was true in World War II. Some, of course, insist that nonviolent resistance with an emphasis on its moral force would eventually win the day.

Some are convinced that the Mohandas Gandhi approach of nonresistance along with civil disobedience is the proper response. Gandhi's crusade would not have been necessary had the British relinquished control of India voluntarily since the occupation violated the standards proposed by Grotius. The motion picture celebrating the life and thesis of Gandhi is somewhat misleading. The reason the endeavors of Gandhi succeeded in India lay in the nature of the British mind. The Christian inheritance came into play here. Britain was no longer capable of using the force demanded by the situation to curb the activities of Gandhi. Had the British acted in the Indian situation as the Soviet Union has acted in Afghanistan, the outcome would have been quite different. And if the people of Afghanistan were not using what force they have to counter the Soviet invasion, that nation would be completely subjugated today. It is the continuing resistance which the Soviets fight to eliminate that keeps the pot boiling. The desire for freedom in this instance is greater than the desire for peace. And death is looked upon as better than slavery.

Recognizing Sin and Evil
The Bible and history demonstrate that man is defective. Faith in Jesus Christ makes a difference, but even Christians are not perfected in this life. Nor is it probable that all men will become Christians before the return of Jesus Christ. The world will always have unbelievers. Sin will abound, and evil will remain until the consummation when Christ will be victor over Satan and evil will be removed from this planet and the cosmos forever. Whatever we do to eliminate the nuclear threat and other threats of force must take into consideration the fact that sin and evil will continue and that not all people will come under the sovereignty of Jesus Christ in this age. Some are so twisted and perverted that they resort to any means to accomplish their evil intentions. The best that we can hope for is to reduce the number of wars and use every means to humanize war in whatever way we can when it does occur. Most of all, we must work to eliminate such devices as nuclear weaponry and death rays.

Christians who accept biblical revelation have another reason for hope in a desperately sick world. They accept the work of the Holy Spirit among people and nations. The Spirit is the Restrainer who keeps men and nations under divine control. They can only go as far as the Holy Spirit will allow.

We cannot forget that Satan, the great enemy of God, is at work in this universe and on this planet. The same one who seduced Adam and wrought all manner of evil in the past is active today. We wrestle not against flesh and blood but against principalities and powers, against the rulers of the darkness of this age (Ephesians 6:12). This spiritual warfare between God and Satan is being fought in the unseen world, and even heaven itself is the scene of this struggle.

A day will come shortly before the consummation when the restraining power of the Holy Spirit will be lifted. When unregenerate men are left to themselves, they do frightful things. Of this we can be sure. When this time comes, they may use nuclear bombs and even death rays, but they will not erase all life from this planet. Fortunately the period of time is short during which these great evils will prevail. And it too is under control of a sovereign God.

God has given us his commandments. He has set before us the issues of life and death. He has stated the consequences, depending on which option we choose. We know what we ought to do; it remains for us to do it. As Christians we are to be the light of the world and salt, to seek peace and pursue it, to pray for those in authority, to work for freedom, peace, and the establishment of righteousness. We are to do these whether we succeed or fail in attaining them.

For Christians the most significant need is to think Christianly. This is difficult to do, but when it is done it changes attitudes, alters the direction we take, and brings healing to men and nations. To think Christianly is nothing more and nothing less than to think the thoughts of Christ. At this point we must face the question whether thinking Christianly allows for war or requires pacifism.

4

War in the Old Testament

Is war permissible for the Christian? This basic question can be settled only by referring to the Bible, which is the source of Christian religious knowledge and the only rule of faith (what we are to believe) and practice (how we are to conduct ourselves).

Some Christians are pacifists or advocates of nonresistance. They are few when compared to the total Christian community, but they are sincere and devout. One respects their convictions, but it still remains to be shown whether their convictions can be sustained from the teaching of the Bible.

Others who have no Christian convictions are pacifists. There are people in the United States who are not governed by the Bible, nor do they profess the Christian faith, for a variety of reasons. They may be atheists, agnostics, practitioners of non-Christian ethnic faiths, or they may be cultists. Although these people are entitled to hold to their viewpoint, the United States became a nation under the rubric of the Judeo-Christian tradition, and an examination of this tradition becomes necessary when we talk about war. For those in the Judaic family the Old Testament is the court of last resort. For Christians, both the Old and the New Testaments apply.

We cannot suppose, if Scripture is normative, that the Old Testament affords insights which are overthrown or reversed by the New Testament. The two Testaments are complementary, not contradictory. It is true, of course, that some of the Old Testament traditions are no longer binding on the Christian community. The dietary laws and the offering of animal sacrifices have been superseded by the Incarnation. Some of those rules which the Old Testament saints were commanded to obey are no longer to be enforced. This does not constitute a reversal but a cessation, and is consistent with progressive revelation. The use of a police force for the preservation of peace at home and the waging of war against external nations and powers does not fit into the category of traditions which have changed by reason of progressive revelation.

From the Old Testament a compelling case can be made for the proposition that God sanctioned war. Capital punishment was used for such crimes as murder and adultery. And it is plain that war as it relates to enemies from without was supported by divine sanction. Pacifism or nonresistance are not found in the Old Testament.

Defensive War
One of the first incidents of war recorded in the Old Testament occurred when Lot and his family were taken captive. Abraham and 318 trained men in his small army pursued the enemy to free Lot and his family. Abraham not only delivered Lot and his family, but he also rescued Lot's goods. As Abraham returned he encountered Melchizedek, a priest of God, who exclaimed: "Blessed be God most high, who has delivered your enemies into your hand" (Genesis 14:20). This war was defensive in nature. Although Abraham seized what the enemy had taken from Sodom and Gomorrah, he refused to keep anything for himself.

God also delivered Israel from the Pharaohs and planned to settle his people in the land of Canaan where the inhabitants of the land had to be dispossessed. Biblical revelation teaches us that God is sovereign and that all of the planet earth belongs to him by right of creation. As the sovereign Lord of the planet, God has the right to give it to whom he pleases and under whatever conditions he wishes. God exercises this prerogative in connection with the inhabitants of Canaan, whose lands he chose to give to Israel.

Moses stated that the commission he gave to Israel was from God, not from himself.

> Now the Lord spoke to Moses in the plains of Moab by the Jordan, across from Jericho, saying, "Speak to the children of Israel, and say to them: 'When you have crossed the Jordan into the land of Canaan, then you shall drive out all the inhabitants of the land from before you, destroy all their engraved stones, destroy all their molded images, and demolish all their high places; you shall dispossess the inhabitants of the land and dwell in it, for I have given you the land to possess.' " (Deuteronomy 33:50-53)

Some scholars have reacted against the commands of God to dispossess people and to kill them. Years ago Bishop G. Bromley Oxnam said that a God who would do this is a "dirty bully" and that in relation to a God who would do this he was an atheist. More recently, Stephen T. Davis in his book *The Debate About the Bible* wrote:

> I speak for no one except myself, but I believe that killing innocent people is morally wrong. And killing Canaanite civilians is to be sharply distinguished from killing Canaanite soldiers in the battles that were necessary for the Israelites to conquer the land that God had promised them. I frankly find it difficult to believe it was God's will that every Canaanite— man, woman, and child—be slaughtered. Since the Bible clearly says that this was God's will, I must conclude that the Biblical writers in this case were mistaken.[1] [See here Joshua 10:40 and 11:20.]

Dr. Davis seems to distinguish between soldiers and civilians and does not say that war itself was not in accord with the will of God. But when one part of the command is divorced from another, does this not raise the question whether any part of the command really came from God?

Some may raise still another question. Why didn't God solve this problem another way? Couldn't he have sent a plague to kill all the people? Why did he command Israel to do what required armed force to succeed? In the book of Joshua we learn that Israel already had an army in its wilderness journeys. "For the people of Israel walked forty years in the wilderness, till all the nation, *the men of war* [my italics] that came forth out of Egypt, perished, because they did not hearken to the voice of the Lord" (Joshua 5:6). Most adult males served in the armed forces. Israel's army was present at the destruction of Jericho, the first enemy city the Israelites took after crossing the River Jordan. We read that as the Israelites marched around the surrounded city of Jericho, they were instructed to "let the armed men pass on before the ark of the Lord" (Joshua 6:8). On the seventh day of the military campaign against Jericho the priests blew the trumpets and Joshua said to the people, "Shout, for the Lord has given you the city" (6:16). When the city was taken, "they utterly destroyed all in the city, both men and women, young and old, oxen, sheep, and asses, with the edge of the sword" (6:21). God had promised Israel the city, and Joshua claimed the promises of God when the walls of the city fell. It is impossible to leave God out of the military investment of Jericho or to proclaim that he had nothing to do with it.

When Nations Deny God

Israel's invasion of Canaan raises the question, Are there times when aggression is legitimate? According to the Grotius principles, no nation is to take what belongs to another nation. The difference here is that it was a sovereign God who commanded Israel to seize these lands. The justice of the act is based on the righteousness of God who executes vengeance on men and nations when they flout his rules and deny his control over them. Shall not the Judge of the whole earth do right?

The taking of Jericho involves the same problem mentioned by Dr. Davis. The command to kill the inhabitants included infants as well as adults.

William E. May, associate professor of moral theology at the Catholic University in Washington, D.C., wrote a letter to the editor in connection with Michael Novak's essay "Moral

Clarity in the Nuclear Age." Professor May said Novak's approach was seriously flawed as to the morality of deterrence and then made this flat statement: "It is absolutely immoral to choose to kill innocent persons, innocent in the technical sense that they are noncombatants."² Surely one would have to agree that the infants in Jericho were noncombatants and thus innocent according to Professor May. There are other moral theologians who would disagree with Professor May. His view may be questioned for several reasons. One is that there are no innocent people—all are conceived in iniquity and born in sin. If God chooses to execute divine judgment on infants, it must be remembered that they are no less guilty than adults.

God's Military Instructions
In the case of Ai, God not only ordered the destruction of the city, but also gave military instructions as to how it was to be accomplished. We read:

> Then the Lord said to Joshua: "Do not be afraid, nor be dismayed; take all the people of war with you, and arise, go up to Ai. See, I have given into your hand the king of Ai, his people, his city and his land. And you shall do to Ai and its king as you did to Jericho and its king. Only its spoil and its cattle you shall take as booty for yourselves. *Lay an ambush for the city behind it*" [my italics]. (Joshua 8:1, 2)

We cannot deny the active participation of God in action. We also read, "The Lord said to Joshua, 'Stretch out the spear that is in your hand toward Ai, for I will give it into your hand.' And Joshua stretched out the spear that he had in his hand toward the city" (Joshua 8:18). Ai fell and the city and its inhabitants were destroyed.

A number of other incidents are connected with the period when Moses and Joshua were Israel's leaders. During the wilderness journey, the Amalekites attacked the Israelites. At Rephidim Moses commanded Joshua: "Choose us some men, and go out, fight with Amalek. Tomorrow I will stand on the top of the hill with the rod of God in my hand" (Exodus 17:8,

9). So long as Moses held up his hand, the Israelites prevailed. When he let it down, the Amalekites were powerful. Aaron and Hur helped Moses hold up his hands, and God gave Israel the victory.

In Deuteronomy the victory of the Israelites over the Amorites is recorded. Sihon, king of Heshbon, would not allow the Israelites to pass through his territory peacefully. God commanded Moses to war against Sihon. Moses noted that "the Lord our God delivered him over to us; so we defeated him, his sons, and all his people. We took all his cities at that time, and we utterly destroyed the men, women, and little ones of every city; we left none remaining" (Deuteronomy 2:33, 34). God was very much involved in this war. He hardened the heart of Sihon. He ordered Moses to take the cities and destroy all life. And Moses obeyed the command of God.

In Numbers we read about the vengeance of God against the Midianites. "And the Lord spoke to Moses, saying: 'Take vengeance for the children of Israel on the Midianites. Afterward you shall be gathered to your people.' So Moses spoke to the people, saying, 'Arm some of yourselves for the war, and let them go against the Midianites to take vengeance for the Lord on Midian. A thousand from each tribe of all the tribes of Israel you shall send to the war'" (Numbers 31:1-4). Israel won the victory, but it came about by war.

In Deuteronomy 20 Moses lays down the laws of war. His injunctions included details relating to male military service. He specified that in sieges fruit-bearing trees were not to be destroyed. He allowed for forced labor by some of the conquered peoples. But he was careful to give definite instructions concerning some of the nations which occupied the land of Canaan. He said:

> Thus you shall do to all the cities which are very far from you, which are not cities of the nations here. But in the cities of these peoples that the Lord your God gives you for an inheritance, you shall save alive nothing that breathes, but you shall utterly destroy them, the Hittites and the Amorites, the Canaanites and the Perizzites, the Hivites and the Jebu-

sites, as the Lord your God has commanded; that they may not teach you to do all their abominable practices which they have done in the service of their gods, and so to sin against the Lord your God. (Deuteronomy 20:15-18)

In Joshua 9 we read that when the kings beyond the Jordan learned of the advance of the Israelites toward their territories, "they gathered together to fight with Joshua and Israel with one accord" (v. 2). This balance of power principle is still used in international politics. It is seen in the NATO and Warsaw pacts, for example. The implications regarding the use of this principle require further analysis when it comes to the prevention of war. In the Joshua account, the military alliance among the nations that feared the advent of Israel served no useful purpose. God had ordained that Israel would defeat the alliance and the land of Canaan would become the possession of his people. God was again directly involved in the history of the nations and in control of their destinies. In the war against the Gibeonites, Joshua "and all the people of war with him, and all the mighty men of valor" (Joshua 10:7) went to battle. "The Lord routed [the Gibeonites] before Israel, killed them with a great slaughter" (10:10). Then God caused great hailstones to kill even more of the enemy than had the Israelites.

The Kingdom Age
Wars were fought continuously during the period of the judges, following the seizure of Canaan by the Israelites. Then Saul became the first king of Israel. Toward the end of Saul's kingship David was in the process of building an army. "Now these were the men who came to David at Ziklag while he was still a fugitive from Saul the son of Kish; and they were among the mighty men, helpers in the war, armed with bows, using both the right hand and the left in hurling stones and shooting arrows with the bow" (1 Chronicles 12:1, 2). Shortly after this, "the Spirit [that is, the Holy Spirit of God, the third person of the Trinity] came upon Amasai, chief of the captains, and he said: 'We are yours, O David; we are on your side, O son of Jesse! Peace, peace to you, and peace to your helpers! For your

God helps you' " (1 Chronicles 12:18). "So David received them and made them captains of the troop." All of this was of God who had promised David that the kingdom would be his and that Saul would be defeated and die. Saul was guilty of disobedience, after which God's judgment was meted out and Saul lost his life. The Holy Spirit of God was at work in this incident and again demonstrates how the sovereign God is involved in the ongoing history of his people and of the world.

God Promises Victory
Before David warred against the Philistines, he inquired of God, "Shall I go up against the Philistines? Will you deliver them into my hand?" God's response was: "Go up, for I will deliver them into your hand" (1 Chronicles 14:10). David knew that victory or defeat was determined by God. He wanted the will of God for himself and for the nation. God told David that he would deliver the Philistines into David's hands. "God has gone before you to strike the camp of the Philistines" (v. 15).

David's life comprised one military campaign after another. God preserved him in all of this (1 Chronicles 18:6) and extended the Israelite kingdom until it reached its zenith. This was accomplished in accord with the will of God and under the protection of God—and it was done militarily.

One other war in the life of David deserves consideration. This was a civil war fought between the armies of David and his son Absalom. Again God was involved. "The Lord had purposed to defeat the good counsel of Ahithophel, to the intent that the Lord might bring disaster on Absalom" (2 Samuel 17:14). In the final battle Absalom was killed, much to David's distress. Yet it was God's way to recover David's throne which had been usurped by his own son.

God's Participation
During the Kingdom Age God himself sometimes warred against the enemies of Israel and wrought destruction. Two such incidents illustrate this truth. The first episode took place during the reign of Jehosphaphat, the king of Judah. A military alliance among the Moabites, Ammonites, and Meunites was

forged against him. Jehoshaphat, fully aware of the danger, expected the enemy to devastate his land. When he learned of the impending invasion, he called for divine help. His prayer, recorded in 2 Chronicles 20:5-12, is a model which all Christians should emulate when in trouble. God sent a prophet, Jahaziel, upon whom the Spirit of God had come in mighty power (2 Chronicles 20:14). God told the prophet to inform Jehosphaphat, "You will not need to fight in this battle. Position yourselves, stand still and see the salvation of the Lord, who is with you, O Judah and Jerusalem. Do not fear or be dismayed; tomorrow go out against them, for the Lord is with you" (2 Chronicles 20:17).

Judah did not raise an arm or shoot an arrow in the battle. God alone defeated the enemies, who fought and destroyed each other. Jehoshaphat and his people came to take away the spoils from a battle they didn't fight. The Bible says that "the fear of God was on all the kingdoms of those countries, when they heard that the Lord had fought against the enemies of Israel. Then the realm of Jehoshaphat was quiet, for his God gave him rest all around" (2 Chronicles 20:29, 30).

The second incident depicts God's war against Sennacherib during the reign of Hezekiah. Sennacherib, king of Assyria, sent his troops to invade Judah and take the city of Jerusalem. Meanwhile, his emissaries delivered a message to convince the people of Judah that resistance was useless:

> Now therefore, do not let Hezekiah deceive you or persuade you like this, and do not believe him; for no god of any nation or kingdom was able to deliver this people from my hand or the hand of my fathers. How much less will your God deliver you from my hand? (2 Chronicles 32:15).

The account of the Sennacherib incident is also recorded in 2 Kings 19 and in Isaiah 37. Hezekiah's prayer is somewhat similar to that of Jehoshaphat, who acknowledged that his eyes were upon God, for he did not know what to do. Hezekiah ends his prayer the same way Jehoshaphat ended his. He prayed: "Now therefore, O Lord our God, I pray, save us from his hand, that all the kingdoms of the earth may know that you are the Lord God, you alone" (2 Kings 19:19). God heard and answered that prayer by divine intervention. Hezekiah was militarily unable to win the victory, but this did not limit God. The outcome was nothing short of miraculous. God sent an angel who killed 185,000 of Sennacherib's troops. Shortly after this, Sennacherib himself was slain by two of his own sons, Adrammelech and Sharezer.

God's Impartial Judgments

We also can conclude that God was impartial in that he rendered adverse judgment against Israel, his own people, when they sinned against him. In Deuteronomy we read how far-reaching the judgments of God are and the consequences of Israel's wickedness:

> And it shall be, that just as the Lord rejoiced over you to do you good and multiply you, so the Lord will rejoice over you to destroy you and bring you to nothing; and you shall be plucked from off the land which you go to possess. Then the Lord will scatter you among the people, from one end of the earth to the other, and there you shall serve other gods, which neither you nor your fathers have known—wood and stone. And among those nations you shall find no rest, nor shall the sole of your foot have a resting place; but there the Lord will give you a trembling heart, failing eyes, and anguish of soul. Your life shall hang in doubt before you; you shall have fear day and night, and have no assurance of life. In the morning you shall say, 'Oh, that it were evening!' And at evening you shall say, 'Oh, that it were morning!' because of the fear which terrifies your heart, and because of the sight which your eyes see (Deuteronomy 28:63-67).

The Israelites know by experience, even to this present day, what the judgments of God are like. And these judgments will continue until the Jews turn to the Messiah whom they have rejected. As soon as they turn back to God, divine deliverance will come.

When nations wage war, no matter who the people are or

whether the war is defensive or constitutes aggression, the purposes and plans of God cannot be annulled. God knows what will transpire before it happens. He bends events so that the ends glorify him and work out his will. Unjust wars have a purpose in God's grand design, even though evil men who wage illegitimate war are unaware of the fact that they are, as it were, pawns in God's hands. Their innermost thoughts are known by him.

The facts reveal that the worst of men are bridled by God so that they cannot go beyond the limits he sets for them. His Spirit loosens and tightens the reins either to pull men up short or let them go further until the moment comes for God to bring their activities to a halt by rendering judgment or eliminating them from his scheme of things as he wishes. Adolf Hitler went as far as God allowed him to go. But the time came when Adolf Hitler was removed from his seat of power, and his empire which he thought would last a thousand years crumbled to dust amid the ruins of Germany, marking the end of the Third Reich.

We have seen in the instances recorded in the Old Testament that war was both defensive and offensive, but was always related to the justice and judgment of God in dealing with mankind's sin. Sometimes God used wicked nations to punish Israel and sometimes he set them down to Israel's advantage. Whatever God's intervention, it was to accomplish his purposes—to resist those who opposed him. We must remember that wherever evil exists, God must wage a war against it. In the case of the Canaanite nations where cities were destroyed and "innocents" died, their leaders opposed God and were punished.

We must also keep in mind that in the same Old Testament God points us toward the day when war will be no more (Micah 4:3).

In both the cosmos and the earth, a great war is being waged between God and Satan. Good and bad angels are involved in this struggle. This war will not cease until Satan has been finally defeated and consigned to the lake of fire, from whence he will never rise to torment men or nature again.

5

The View from the New Testament

The New Testament, so far as the words of Jesus are concerned, affords us no explicit statement of approval or disapproval of war per se. Nowhere are Christians forbidden to serve in the armed forces, nor are they prohibited from occupying the office of magistrate. But some people interpret certain of the sayings of Jesus to prohibit such activity.

In the Sermon on the Mount, as recorded in the Gospel of Matthew, we read:

> You have heard that it was said, "An eye for an eye and a tooth for a tooth." But I tell you not to resist an evil person. But whoever slaps you on your right cheek, turn the other to him also. If anyone wants to sue you and take away your tunic, let him have your cloak also. And whoever compels you to go one mile, go with him two. Give to him who asks you, and from him who wants to borrow from you do not turn away. (5:38-42)

This Scripture refers to our personal relationships. In general we may say that if someone does wrong to me, his act does not give me license to do wrong to him. Two wrongs do not make a right. It is not the will of God for me to slap my neighbor in return when he slaps me for no good reason. If I am sued by someone who wants my tunic, I am to give him my cloak as well. In other words, I am to work for peace with my neighbor even if it costs me something or even if I have done him no wrong to begin with. Obviously if I have wronged a brother I should make it right, and he should not have to sue me to obtain a settlement. "How far this principle can be applied to groups, and especially to political life, is constantly debated."[1] To employ proper hermeneutical principles, one should avoid claiming that this Scripture *explicitly* supports the nonresistance or pacifist positions. It does not. Eisegesis (the interpretation of a text by reading into it one's own ideas) is a constant and present danger for all who earnestly study the Bible and never consciously misuse the Bible.

It is clear, however, that in this instance Jesus is saying nothing about the conduct of nations. He is talking to those who are his followers. No Christian nation existed in the world at that time, nor is there one today. When an unbelieving and aggressor nation overruns another nation and kills its people, it surely is not the intent of Jesus to tell the nation that has been overrun to sit still and invite the aggressor to kill them off one by one. That would be to commit suicide, and suicide is wrong. When aggressors wantonly kill others, they are defacing the image of God in those they kill. Why would it not be proper for the victims to resist the aggressor to preserve the image of God and to prevent wickedness from triumphing?

Later in Matthew we read these words of Jesus: "Do not think that I came to bring peace on earth. I did not come to bring peace but a sword." According to *The Interpreter's Bible*, "the main import of these words is not literal. The confession of Christ has brought in actuality the sword of persecution; and there has been behind our wars a conflict of life views, one being more Christian than the other. But there is no justification here for the war method—not while the Sermon on the Mount remains."[2] In other words, Jesus' use of the sword is not to be taken literally. This is somewhat strained, since it would have been quite easy for Jesus to have used another word that would not support the notion that war by the sword is not really war by the sword. Yet, Jesus did say, in the Sermon on the Mount, "Blessed are the peacemakers, for they shall be called sons of God" (Matthew 5:9). How do we reconcile these two Scriptures?

Again quoting *The Interpreter's Bible:* "[The peacemaker's] fundamental work is always to reconcile men with God. For as long as men are at odds with God, they are at odds with themselves and with their neighbors. Therefore the true evangelist is the best peacemaker: he pleads that men shall turn to Christ, who himself breaks down 'the middle wall of partition' (Ephesians 2:14), thus making peace. So the most important work of the peacemaker is the practice of the presence of God. Through that communion the peacemaker can give peace from the overflow of his own peace-filled heart."[3] With this we can all agree.

Commenting on the same verse, Matthew Henry wrote: "By this it appears that Christ never intended to have his religion propagated by fire and sword, or penal laws, or to acknowledge bigotry, or intemperate zeal, as the mark of his disciples."[4]

Striving for Peace

Nowhere does the Bible suggest that the gospel be preached by using the sword. The evangelist, whether he preaches at home or abroad, should not ever use force of any kind to spread the Good News. He is a peacemaker in the best sense of the word. We must ask ourselves, is this Scripture for believers in their personal relations with those they talk to as they share the gospel, or does it mean that international relations are governed by the same principle? Surely we can agree that all should try to solve national and international problems, as well as personal ones, in a peaceful way, but this does not mean that war is forbidden or that it is illicit. War *can* be illicit, but not every use of force is wrong. When peacemakers do not succeed in their efforts, and wicked men start conflicts because they are covetous, just wars become necessary.

Someone suggested to Richard Cobden, the English statesman and economist, that he might attain such fame as to warrant his being buried in Westminster Abbey. To this he replied, "My spirit could not rest in peace among those men of war." Might he not have felt equally uncomfortable if he were laid beside the great heroes listed in Hebrews 11 who were men of war and as such were blessed by God? These included Moses, Gideon, Barak, Samson, Jephthah, and David. Cobden appears to have overlooked how the Bible in the Book of Revelation pictures Jesus Christ as a warrior, coming to win the battle of Armageddon and to finish the divine war against Satan and all evil. John wrote:

> Then I saw heaven opened, and behold, a white horse. And he who sat on him was called Faithful and True, and in righteousness he judges and makes war. His eyes were like a flame of fire, and on his head were many crowns. He had a name written that no one knew except himself. He was clothed with a robe dipped in blood and his name is called the Word of God. And the armies in heaven, clothed in fine linen, white and clean, followed him on white horses. Now out of his mouth goes a sharp sword, that with it he should strike the nations. And he himself will rule them with a rod of iron. He himself treads the winepress of the fierceness and wrath of Almighty God. And he has on his robe and on his thigh a name written: KING OF KINGS AND LORD OF LORDS. (Revelation 19:11-16)

A day will come when peace in the cosmos will be restored, but only after Christ has defeated Satan, the author of sin and war. He is the one who makes resistance and just wars necessary until the end of the age and the coming triumph of Christ.

Wars of Aggression

One of the curious aspects of the current nuclear threat involves a substantial segment of the church. At no point has the Russian Orthodox Church lifted its voice against the wars of the Soviet Union—wars of aggression in which they have invaded nations such as Afghanistan, Hungary, Finland, Poland, and Czechoslovakia. The same is true about the National and the World Councils of Churches. No prophetic word has come in criticism of the Soviet Union and its aggressions. They have done nothing significant to counter the Soviet Union's denial of human rights to its own people and those of the captive nations. The National and World Councils of Churches have consistently been critical of the United States and have even judged it to be warlike. At the same time these councils have given money to revolutionary movements around the world and have encouraged wars of revolution against what they call repressive regimes. The so-called Christian liberation theology proponents also call for revolution to destroy free enterprise and bring socialism in its place. They are not peacemakers in the biblical sense of that term.

Among the leaders of the theology of liberation movement in Latin America are such men as Rubem Alves, Gustavo Gutierrez, Juan Luis Segundo, Hugo Assman, Camilo Torres, and Helder Camara. Many of their works have been published by Orbis Press, a Roman Catholic publisher which represents the leftists in the Roman Catholic Church. The same leftist emphasis is found among the clergy of the Roman Catholic Church in Latin America. Protestants also are involved in the revolutionary movement south of the United States. One of the best known is Jose Miguez-Bonino of Argentina, a Methodist and former president of the World Council of Churches. Miguez-Bonino has written several books, including *Christians and Marxists: The Mutual Challenge to Revolution*. He claimed that he was writing as a Christian.

> As a Latin American Christian I am convinced—with many other Latin Americans who have tried to understand the situation of our people and to place it in world perspective— that revolutionary action aimed at changing the basic economic, political, social and cultural structures and conditions of life is imperative today in the world. Ours is not a time for mere development but for basic and revolutionary change (which ought not to be equated necessarily with violence). The possibility for human life to remain human on our planet hangs on our ability to affect this change.[5]

Miguez-Bonino applauded the writings of Juan Rosales, whom he acknowledged to be an Argentine Marxist author. He quoted Rosales as saying that:

The bringing about of a true revolutionary transformation in our country. . . . is for us (Communists) inconceivable without the resolute participation of a renewed and engaged Christianity which is equipped to make its specific contribution to the revolutionary baggage.[6]

Miguez-Bonino also endorsed the statement made by Italian Waldensian Mario Miegge: "I confess that I am a Christian, but I declare myself a Marxist." He also agrees with the Puerto Rican professor of theology who said of Miegge's affirmation, "It should be inconceivable for progressive Christians [to envision a revolution] without the orientating contribution of Marxism-Leninism or without the protagonistic activity of the working class."[7]

Miguez-Bonino enthusiastically endorsed what he called the almost complete "elimination of malnutrition, illiteracy and premature mortality for 800 million people (in mainland China) in less than thirty years." Then he praised the advances made in Cuba under the leadership of Fidel Castro.[8] His classic contribution is contained in a statement taken from the writings of Ernst Bloch about the "red hero":

He confesses up to his death the cause for which he has lived, and clearly, coldly, consciously, he advances toward the Nothingness in which he has learned to believe as a free spirit. His sacrifice is different from that of the ancient martyrs: these died almost without an exception with a prayer on their lips, confident that they had thus merited Heaven. . . . But the Communist hero, whether under the Tsars, under Hitler or under any other power, sacrifices himself without hope of resurrection. His Good Friday is not sweetened—much less absorbed—by any Easter Sunday in which he will personally return to life. The Heaven to which the martyrs raised their arms amidst flames and smoke, does not exist for the red materialist. And nevertheless he dies confessing a cause, and his superiority can only be compared with that of the very early Christians or of John the Baptist.[9]

The acceptance and exaltation of Marxism-Leninism among church leaders constitutes support for the Soviet Union and its satellites, not to mention Communist China as well. There is a conscious or unconscious endeavor to immortalize and to sanctify as heroes people who give themselves with abandonment to the Communist cause. But this brings us back to the person of Jesus and his attitude toward these matters.

Jesus Speaks on Fighting

In addition to the statements of Jesus we have looked at, others should be considered. Jesus appeared before Pontius Pilate, who asked Jesus whether he was the king of the Jews. Jesus' response was, "My kingdom is not of this world. If my kingdom were of this world, my servants would fight, so that I should not be delivered to the Jews; but now my kingdom is not from here" (John 18:36). Jesus distinguishes between the two kingdoms, the kingdom of God and the nation-state system. He acknowledges that in the kingdoms of this world servants are called upon to fight for their kings, and that if his kingdom were of this world his servants would fight. If Jesus disapproved of the use of force, he would have employed different language and made it plain that neither the servants of his kingdom or of the kingdoms of this world should use force. One can only conclude that given the nature of man, force must be used to restrain wickedness, for it will never be accomplished any other way.

One of Jesus' strongest statements was spoken in his famous sermon about the house that is divided and cannot stand. He said:

> When a strong man, fully armed, guards his own palace, his goods are in peace. But when someone stronger than he comes upon him and overcomes him, he takes from him all his armor in which he trusted, and divides his spoils. (Luke 11:21, 22)

The principle here is plain. Peace is best guaranteed by being armed against those who would take from us what we have. Jesus realizes that there are strong enemies who come upon those who are less strong, disarming them and dividing the goods. Why would Jesus use this illustration if in fact he wanted us to do nothing by way of defending ourselves against aggression? The Old Testament shows that on a few occasions God used his supernatural power to deliver Israel, but in most instances Israel was instructed to fight against the enemies. Nothing in the New Testament directs either men or nations to leave themselves open to destruction by refusing to take protective action as the strong man did in this illustration of Jesus.

The true pacifist is faced with inconsistencies, for he does not and indeed cannot carry through on his pacifism in every regard. Few if any pacifists leave their doors unlocked at night. A lock is a form of armament—a deterrent which has for its chief purpose keeping people out. Would not consistent pacifism preclude the office of policeman too? Some in the peace camp refuse to pay taxes which support police power. To be totally consistent, pacifists would have to establish their own communities, totally unrelated to government and free from entanglements which produce inconsistencies. Scripture does not suggest this, however. Rather, the opposite is true. Though Jesus said we are not of this world, he sent us back into the world to serve and to witness. In his prayer Jesus said that as the Father had sent him into the world, "I also have sent them into the world" (John 17:18).

Jesus and Government

Jesus also paid the temple tax and taught us to render unto Caesar the things that are Caesar's. This meant that Christians in that day were to pay taxes that made it possible for Caesar to maintain his armed forces. From this we see that support of armed might is not in itself wrong.

The appeal to the words of Jesus in the New Testament for the support of the pacifist position requires one further elaboration. It is needed because the pacifist position is essentially a claim based on what its adherents believe about the New Testament but not about the Old Testament. Unless one wishes to demythologize the Old Testament or eliminate those portions that expressly declare that God ordered the annihilation of certain peoples, it appears that the Old Testament and the New Testament are at variance with each other on this question. But this cannot be, for Scripture does not contradict itself. Jesus Christ is the same yesterday, today, and forever. Neither can there be disagreement among the members of the Trinity. We read about God in the Old Testament, which also embraces Jesus Christ and the Holy Spirit. The members of the Trinity are always in agreement.

In the light of this, one other fact must be looked at. Rene Padilla, a contribution editor to *Sojourners* magazine, wrote, "The fact remains, however, that there is no just war. . . . The task that those of us who confess Christ as our Lord have before us is to denounce the crime of war and announce the gospel of peace."[10] If there is no just war, then the wars ordered by God were unjust. Ergo, God is an unjust God because he ordered Israel to do what Dr. Padilla says is unjust. In addition, one would have to say that the war which Jesus will conduct when he returns in glory to destroy the enemies of God must also be unjust.

It would appear that the teachings of Jesus do not explicitly support the pacifist or nonresistance positions. In the light of Jesus' Trinitarian relationship, it seems that he could not take a pacifist position unless he were to repudiate his own involvement in the acts of God with regard to war in the Old Testament.

The Apostles and War

Almost half of the books of the New Testament (thirteen out of twenty-seven) were written by Paul, but they do not include extensive treatment on the subject of war. They do, however, reflect his personal practice and attitudes toward government, and set forth instructions for us.

Paul was proud of the fact that he was a Roman citizen and mentions it several times, as recorded in the Acts of the Apostles, written by Luke. He did not hesitate to claim the rights which pertained to that citizenship when it seemed judicious to do so. Although the Roman government was pagan,

Paul never passed adverse judgment on it. Nor did he say Christians ought not be part of it, or that they should revolt against it. Undoubtedly he was aware of the teaching of Jesus to render to God what is God's and to Caesar what is Caesar's. This meant that when there was a conflict between the demands of Caesar and the demands of God, he was to obey God rather than men. This principle was already part of the apostolic practice. In Acts 5:29 we read that "Peter and the other apostles answered and said: 'We ought to obey God rather than men.' " Whatever God has commanded must take precedence over what men demand. At the same time Paul carefully told Titus: "Remind them to be subject to rulers and authorities, to obey, to be ready for every good work" (Titus 3:1). Since the law of God did not always conflict with the law of Caesar, obedience to the civil power was the duty of every Christian.

Paul's Example

Late in his ministry Paul returned to Jerusalem and was taken prisoner and accused by the Jews of being guilty of sedition. He appeared first before Felix and then before Festus, because sedition was a criminal offense against the Roman government. When Paul argued his case before Festus, he claimed that "neither against the law of the Jews, nor against the temple, nor against Caesar have I offended in anything at all" (Acts 25:8). When Festus, wanting to appease the Jews, asked Paul whether he was willing to go up to Jerusalem to be judged, he responded in the negative by saying: "I stand at Caesar's judgment seat where I ought to be judged. To the Jews I have done no wrong, as you very well know. For if I am an offender, or have committed anything worthy of death, I do not object to dying; but if there is nothing in these things of which these men accuse me, no one can deliver me to them. I appeal to Caesar" (Acts 25:10, 11).

Paul, in this statement, conveys four truths. He certified that the government of Rome was a legal government and had the right to try him. He accepted capital punishment as a suitable penalty for sedition. He agreed that any Christian who was a seditionist was guilty under Roman law and could be punished. He was in agreement that the power of the sword rested in the hands of the Roman government, so that the government itself would be committing no crime if and when it executed him for the crime of which he was accused, if he were to be found guilty. He backed the idea of police power for the state. If the state has police power to deal with internal affairs and to execute judgment against its own citizenry, it also has the power of armed might in connection with external enemies who threaten the state.

Paul's Teaching

In Paul's writing to the Romans we know he had in mind their government. We do well to remember that he said the Roman emperor was "God's minister to you for good" (Romans 13:4). Government is ordained by God for our good, and we are to obey it. This does not mean that any particular government is always good or that there are no bad governments. When governments are so bad that obedience to them conflicts with the law of God, then we are to resist that kind of government. No government will be perfect, because no man is perfect. But imperfection of government does not release Christians from responsibility to government. When it is basically corrupt, however, and defies the moral law of God, that is a different matter.

In the case of Rome, the situation worsened after the church gained numbers and strength. Religious freedom was curtailed because emperor-worship prevailed. Christians had no choice except to disobey when called upon to offer sacrifices to the emperor. Wherever religious freedom is annulled, the abridgment of other basic human rights also occurs. Christians must resist government which functions in this manner. From the biblical standpoint such resistance, to enjoy the blessing of God, must have for its objective a new government based upon the freedoms called for under the rubric of general revelation.

In writing to the Romans, Paul also affirmed police power. Any state that functions under the common laws which nature itself requires has the duty to resist those who break these laws. When men make their own laws and break the laws of others with impunity, and when there is no general law covering all of the citizenry, society breaks down and anarchy takes over. No state can survive when anarchy prevails. Even a condition in which imperfection abounds is less evil then unmitigated anarchy when no one is safe from his nearest neighbor.

Paul carefully speaks of the ruler not only as God's minister, but as God's avenger "to execute wrath on him who practices evil" (Romans 13:4). When Paul here speaks of evil, he can only have in mind those things which are contrary to the law of God. Sometimes the state may declare something to be evil which God declares to be good. When this inversion occurs, the state has no right to demand obedience and the citizen under God's law cannot obey. In such a case the Christian suffers for righteousness' sake. On the other hand, when he suffers for that which is unrelated to unrighteousness, then he has no right to complain. He deserves the punishment which is meted out to him.

The apostle also commands Christians to pay their taxes. He offers no exception to this rule. He does not say to pay taxes for certain expenses of the government, such as police protection, and to refuse to pay taxes for the support of the armed forces. If a pacifist today refuses to pay taxes for the support of the police power, he receives benefits of protection without sharing the cost of those benefits—which in itself has moral implications.

The United States is founded on a Constitution which is a compact agreeable to the people who have established the Constitution by which they are governed. The Congress of the United States is specifically enjoined to exercise its power under Article I, Section 8 to declare war, to raise and support armies, to provide and maintain a navy, and to make rules for the government and regulation of the land and naval forces. The president, the members of Congress, and the members of the Supreme Court take an oath of allegiance which includes the promise to protect and obey the Constitution. Any pacifist or nonresistance person elected or appointed to any of these offices cannot take such an oath and remain consistent with his convictions. He is faced with one of two choices: either he must forsake his convictions, or fail to do his duty in accord with his oath of office. The ethical implications of pacifism under such circumstances are important, for if a man will break his oath either way he is morally suspect in other areas of life.

No one can claim that Paul's teaching in the New Testament advocates or defends pacifism. A fair exegetical approach to his teaching leads us in one direction: the police power of the state for internal and external protection exists, but it must be employed within the context of the total revelation of God in the Bible.

What about the writings of Peter on this subject? In 1 Peter 2 we read, "Submit yourselves to every ordinance of man for the Lord's sake, whether to the king as supreme, or to governors, as to those who are sent by him for the punishment of evildoers and for the praise of those who do good" (vv. 13, 14). He was writing to believers. In mentioning rulers meting out punishment to those who are evildoers, he too affirms the police power of the state. The context here has to do primarily with internal police power rather than power between states.

The Need for Police Power

The Bible, both in the Old and New Testaments, allows for police power among men and nations. The need for such power arises from the evil nature of men, which requires restraints and penalties. Although we have been given principles, we are not provided with details about what to do in every circumstance. These are for us to decide. The nuclear bomb problem is a relatively new one in international relations and one which will not soon disappear. How to deal with this problem faces all mankind at this time. The issue takes on its significance from the quantitative aspect of its power. When weighed against former conventional weaponry, it makes destruction possible beyond any moral calculation. A reasonable approach to nuclear power in war would be to destroy all nuclear weaponry. How this feat could be accomplished is less easily determined than the fact that ideally it ought to be achieved. This brings us to a consideration of what the policies of the United States should be and how we should work to make nuclear war impossible.

6

The Enemy

For years the Soviet Union has spent a greater proportion of its annual wealth on armaments than has the United States, making it the world's most powerful nation militarily.

The Soviet Union and the United States represent two totally different systems which are engaged in a worldwide struggle for supremacy. The United States would not need to fear a peaceful Socialist experiment, nor would there be any reason to build a military machine with fearful potential destructive power if the Soviet Union was a peaceful nation. The United States could face any competition from the U.S.S.R. in the economic realm, but when force is an integral factor of the Russian economic system and the nation proclaims that its single great objective is the destruction of what it calls imperialism, and when it points to the United States as the leading imperialist nation, the issue is joined.

The enemy we face is not the great masses of people in the Soviet Union. We distinguish the ruled from the rulers, the common people from the autocratic minority comprising the Communist leadership in the Kremlin. The people of the Soviet Union want peace as much as the people of America and Western Europe want peace, but the people of the Soviet Union are oppressed by a system ruled by determined bosses whose intention is to control the world. The masters of the Kremlin now control the media, the economic processes, and the very lives of the people. The common man is terrorized, brainwashed, and kept uninformed of what is taking place inside and outside the Soviet Union. Whoever raises questions or dissents from the party line is dealt with by security agencies that are capable of infamous crimes against human beings who do not choose to follow the accepted ideology of the ruling elite. We are fighting for the masses of Soviet people, not against them. They need freedom, but there appears to be little possibility for them to escape the clutches of a totalitarian regime without help from outside their prison. The true battle, then, is against the relatively small group of Marxist-Leninist elite who hold millions of their fellowmen captive.

Since the Soviet Union is the enemy, we must know what the enemy believes. What is the philosophical base that undergirds national life and international operations? It is no secret that the history of the Soviet Union can be understood only within the context of Marxism-Leninism. Just as we can comprehend Hitler's Germany only by reading and understanding *Mein Kampf,* so we need to read the literature of Karl Marx, Friedrich Engels, Nikolai Lenin, and those who have followed them to understand the Soviet Union, what it stands for, and what it intends to do.

Socialism is not a new phenomenon. In Plato's *Republic* it was presented as Utopia. Simply stated, socialism always has for its linchpin the notion that egalitarianism in all areas of life is the proper answer to economic systems in which some are masters and others servants. The Soviet form of socialism, however, is different, for it rests on certain other philosophic foundations which make it distinct from Socialist ideas and experiments in earlier ages. Soviet socialism is based on dialectical materialism.

Atheistic

The materialism of Marxism-Leninism assumes that the ultimate reality is matter, not spirit, making it atheistic. It allows for no God. Only matter is eternal. This separates it from the Judeo-Christian view of the world and life which starts with God instead of matter. Soviet socialism regards religion as the opiate of the people, an invention of man to establish an economic system based on inequality and laden with injustice. A system which considers matter the ultimate reality cannot develop ethics and morality based on any objective and eternal standard, since matter does not have in it the qualities found in theistic views of the world. This notion either has not occurred to the Marxists or they are not deterred by such an idea.

The contribution Karl Marx made to socialism derives from his philosophy, the substance of which was designed to show how the present order came to be and to put forth a plan by which the present order could be abolished and a better one substituted for it. By creating a belief in the ultimate salvation of man on earth, Marx became the progenitor of the largest mass movement since early Christianity and the father of the greatest subversive force in the modern world. In addition to being a materialist, he promoted the concept of the dialectic, which explained not only how things came to be what they are, but what they will lead to in the future. This segment of his philosophy was derived from the philosopher Georg Hegel, but stripped of the theistic element of the Great Mover which was part of Hegel's philosophy of history. It combined the threefold principle of thesis, antithesis, and synthesis. As used by Marx, it explained the various stages of development through which man has progressed: primitive, slaveholding, feudal, capitalism, socialism, and ultimately communism. At each stage in the development of man, the reigning viewpoint, the thesis, was challenged by an antithesis. In the ensuing struggle a synthesis developed which was a new and higher form of development. Marx accepted the fact that in his day capitalism was in the saddle. He said it would give way to socialism and later socialism would give way to communism. This theory has been called the "laws of historical development," thought to be a comprehensive view of history which offers guidance similar to that provided by religion. It can be used as a substitute for religion by those who no longer wish to believe in God.

Foreordained
Marxism looks on this viewpoint of history as operating inexorably in accordance with built-in laws. In the simplest possible

terms, things are foreordained and what is foreordained must surely take place. Understanding this is of the utmost significance in the struggle between the Socialist and the free worlds. The Soviet Union and the Communists as a whole believe that history is on their side. Capitalism *must* perish and socialism *must* prevail. To say that this view is incorrect from the Judeo-Christian standpoint carries no weight with the Marxists. They are convinced that what they believe will take place.

Because of this adherence to the laws of historical development, Marxism must be regarded as a religion. Beliefs tightly knit and closely held command the allegiance of the devotees to such an extent they are willing to die for what they hold to be true. When a sufficient number of people are so motivated, they can be a powerful force in history regardless of the form the "religion" assumes. Witness the fact that Christianity started with a small number of highly motivated and committed disciples of Jesus Christ. In three centuries their numbers had so increased and their power had become so strong, they were able to overcome and conquer the Roman Empire. Literally they turned the world upside-down. They replaced the Greek-Roman culture which had prevailed for centuries. In its place they were able to substitute the Judeo-Christian tradition, which continues to exist although it has been seriously challenged by the Enlightenment which began in the eighteenth century and has flowered in the last half-century.

Marxism has prevailed in many places because so many believe its basic tenets, it is propagated so fervently, and it commands the devotion of its followers. Unless and until it dawns on its adherents that they are wrong or the system has existed long enough for its internal weaknesses to sap Marxism's vitality and weaken the convictions of its practitioners, it will represent a continuing danger to the free world and to those who hold to the capitalist tradition.

State-controlled

In the economic realm Marxism holds that the right of individuals to own and operate the means of production is the essential evil of capitalism. Communism's economic belief is that no individual should own any of the means of production. Rather, all economic activity should be controlled by the state. Public ownership of the means of production does not do away with capitalism; it simply changes its focus. Instead of capitalism, the Communist substitutes state capitalism.

Even under state capitalism, profit (thought to be an evil by the Communists) is essential if the economic conditions of the citizenry are to be improved, but it goes to the state which distributes it whatever way the leadership chooses. No one can own a farm, run a business of any kind, start a bank, publish a newspaper, open a supermarket, or own a taxicab service. Socialism or state capitalism without armed might would present no enduring threat to free enterprise. In the long run it would prove unsuitable for man as he is and would end up in the dustbin of history. Under communism, state capitalism is a threat because of its armed might and the assumption that entrepreneur capitalism must be eliminated from the world. It is the unchanging goal of communism to apply the executioner's axe to capitalism, which is regarded as the enemy of socialism. The attempt to eliminate capitalism (now called imperialism because Marx failed to see that capitalism would reach a higher form of economic life) is part of the Marxist view of history which guarantees in advance that capitalism must die and communism must win the day. It is the duty of every Marxist to wage unceasing warfare against its greatest enemy. They do so because of their faith-belief that victory will be theirs.

Revolutionary

A difference exists between utopian Socialists and Communists. The utopian believes that the victory for socialism will be secured through democratic means. They think people will vote in socialism. The Communists think this to be naivete. They believe and teach that revolution is the means by which their brand of socialism will come into being. This does not mean that the Communists do not wish to win their victory apart from nuclear war. They prefer to employ a variety of methods. One is to create and sustain revolutionary movements wherever capitalism prevails. This methodology has succeeded in places like Cuba, North Korea, and Nicaragua. Marxism is seeking to do the same in European nations through Communist parties which are under the thumb of the Soviet Union.

A second method the Soviet Union employs to overthrow the non-Socialist world is to build a war machine so large and so strong that by threat rather than by direct force they will be able to topple governments opposed to them. The existence of a military machine such as the Soviet Union presently has is a powerful force which motivates multitudes to call for peace at any price and to suppose that it is better to be Red than dead. The possibility of nuclear annihilation, encouraged by the Soviets as a device to win without having to use nuclear weaponry, has spawned a large and vocal pacifist movement around the globe. It does not exist and would not be permitted to exist in any substantial form in the Soviet Union itself, which regards pacifism as a sign of bourgeois decadence. The same threat of nuclear annihilation by the Soviets has called forth a demand by some in the United States for unilateral disarmament. In some nations neutralism is the current rage, based on the supposition that the two major powers, the United States and the Soviet Union, can fight it out with each other and leave the neutral nations to themselves. This optimism is encouraged by the Soviets, for it helps them in their strategy to divide and conquer.

Subversive

A third Soviet device is to arrange for détente with the United States. In every phase of current history, when détente has been in operation it has given the Soviet Union time to enlarge its military capability and to engage in subversive activities in various places. It has led to ventures in South Africa using Cuba as a surrogate. It has brought about the invasion of Afghanistan and the use of chemical warfare to quell a resentful people. During détente the Soviets have penetrated Central America, where right now the United States is labeled the aggressor.

Few Americans are aware of Soviet actions near the shores of the United States, because the news media remain silent, whatever their reasons. Information such as in the following report is found in sources unavailable to the general public.

Navy intelligence has reported that two Soviet warships—a high speed guided-missile cruiser and an anti-submarine frigate—sailed to within *50 miles* of the Mississippi River Delta in January. It was the closest any Soviet warships had come to the United States since they began periodic exercises in the Caribbean and Gulf of Mexico from Cuban ports 14 years ago. None of the Russian vessels have behaved in a provocative manner, as yet. But American defense officials are concerned over the growing boldness of the Soviet "blue water" navy, which now numbers 1,000 ships or about twice the size of the U.S. navy.

The Pentagon still is not talking about the mock attacks on San Diego, Los Angeles and San Francisco staged by three Soviet submarines off the California coast last August. A reliable intelligence source told *America's Future* correspondent Philip C. Clarke that the Soviet subs could have launched nuclear missiles at the three U.S cities with only eight minutes warning, had it been a real attack. The January exercise 50 miles off the coast of Louisiana put the Soviet cruiser *Admiral Isakov* within seconds of New Orleans as the missile flies. This, obviously, is too close for comfort.

Since 1969, the Soviets have sent 22 naval flotillas or squadrons into the Caribbean and the Gulf. Russian warships now operate with increasing frequency from Cuban ports, including the newly-enlarged naval base at Cienfuegos, and conduct joint exercises with the Cuban navy. The Cubans themselves now have the largest navy in Latin America, including four Soviet-built submarines and scores of missile-firing speedboats. All this is in addition to a steadily growing Cuban air force that includes more than 200 Soviet-built MIG's, sharing newly-enlarged bases with long-range Russian reconnaissance bombers.

The Soviets and their Cuban allies have been busy gathering immense amounts of intelligence on U.S. defenses,

or lack of them, and familiarizing themselves with our coast-
lines and shipping lanes. The Soviets know that in the event
of conflict, the United States and its allies would depend on
Caribbean sea lanes for the movement of troops, arms and
supplies. Much of the oil and raw materials for U.S. industry
also must pass through the Caribbean and the Gulf.[1]

All of this should not surprise us. It is entirely consistent
with the world and life-view of communism. It is carrying out
what the philosophy of Marxism requires for the defeat of
capitalism and democracy. No democratic nation in the world
has for its primary purpose the conquest of the globe. Certainly
the United States has nothing like this on its agenda. This does
not mean the United States was not an expanding nation, desir-
ous of increasing its borders. The term "manifest destiny" is
well known to America historians who have recorded the
march of America from the east to the west coat. There were
land purchases such as the Louisiana Purchase and the purchase of Alaska from Czarist Russia. There was a war from
which America gained additional lands from Mexico. In the
Spanish-American War Cuba and the Philippines were taken
from Spain. But that period of American history has ended.
Canada and Mexico have nothing to fear from the United
States. The borders common to both nations are unguarded,
while those which separate the Soviet Union and the People's
Republic of China are lined with armed forces.

Despite the Soviet rhetoric, the major difference between
the United States and the Soviet Union is that the latter is an
expanding, aggressor nation whereas the United States seeks to
protect itself and the borders and integrity of its allies. What
the Soviet Union is doing does not square with its avowal of
peaceful intentions. Its actions cannot cover up or nullify the
basic philosophy which drives the Soviets to revolutionary and
military activities around the world.

Class Struggle
Doing away with private ownership of the means of production
is understood better when it is linked with class struggle—

another premise of Communist thought. Marxism divides the world into two kinds of people—bourgeoisie (the exploiters) and proletariat (the exploited). To destroy capitalism means the end of the bourgeoisie, who are the capitalists, and victory for the proletariat. The history of the world, according to Marxist theory, is the unceasing and irreconcilable struggle between these two classes. Each class is what it is and cannot think or act differently from its nature, which derives from its class. Marx said that private property ownership brought into being the opposition between the two classes. This is not something that pertains to a single nation. It is common to all nations, for the two divergent classes exist around the world. The interests of each class remain the same whether the individuals are English, Spanish, German, Italian, or American.

Marx claimed that these two classes are real social and political forces which act in history, but do not share common values or ideas. They have essentially differing consciousness and must act according to their class interests, resulting in a struggle. According to the Marxists, their rule by the capitalist class is morally wrong and deserves to be destroyed. They say capitalist society is bound to collapse because there are laws operating which lead inevitably to this collapse and its replacement by the dictatorship of the proletariat. Class struggle, therefore, is part of the historical process by which one stage of historical progress gives rise to a higher economic form. From this, Marx and his followers have established the following suppositions:

(1) Marxists have a target: the capitalists.
(2) Marxists have a moral ground for action: capitalism is immoral.
(3) They predict capitalism must and will collapse.

One can ask on what basis they pronounce a moral judgment against capitalism. They have no grounds. They simply affirm this to be true. Since their system denies the possibility of metaphysics, how can there be any reason for Marxists to make this adverse judgment against capitalism?

In the *Communist Manifesto,* written by Marx and Engels, we read, "Communists everywhere support every revolutionary movement against the existing social and political order of things. In all these movements they bring to the front, as the leading question in each, the property question, no matter what degree of development at the time." And they acknowledge "the clearest possible recognition of the hostile antagonism between bourgeoisie and proletariat."

So long as the Communists retain their allegiance to Marxist-Leninist principles they will be the chief enemy of the West, which is capitalist and bourgeois. The nature of their faith demands that they use force to overcome the enemy, which is the West and in particular the United States as the leader of the capitalist world. Were it not for the existence of the Communist menace, the likelihood of nuclear holocaust or conventional war on a worldwide scale would be negligible.

Inhuman

No one has more forcefully spelled out the dangers of the Communist menace than Alexander Solzhenitsyn, who wrote about the Soviet Union and its stance following the death of Brezhnev. Among the points he made were these: "In its inhumanity, communism has no historical precedent. . . . Communism is a trap from which no nation has ever escaped. . . . The main goal of communism is an irrational and fanatical urge to swallow the maximum amount of external territory and population, with the ideal limit being the entire planet. . . . It is a dangerous illusion to draw distinctions between 'better' and 'worse' communisms, between more peaceful and more aggressive kinds. They are all inimical to humanity. . . . It is futile to hope that a compromise with communism will be found, or that relations will be improved by concessions and trade. Communism is a denial of life; it is a fatal disease of a nation and the death of all humanity. . . . A survey of Soviet reality shows, however, that neither a change of leadership nor dozens of symbolic gestures could improve the situation. . . . To improve or to correct communism is not feasible. Communism can only be done away with—by the joint efforts of the many people oppressed by it." So says Solzhenitsyn, whose grasp of the Soviet mentality and his understanding of its intentions exceeds that of those who have not seen the system in operation.

Discovering who the enemy is and on what basis this hostile relationship with the non-Communist world rests is a first step. We must also examine the moral and ethical views of this enemy, for without such understanding we might mistakenly tread a path of illusion which could easily lead to disastrous consequences.

7

Communist Principles

International relationships depend on the nature of the moral and ethical principles by which individuals and nations conduct themselves. When men and nations share common ethical and moral standards, the climate for peace is immeasurably enhanced. Although it is true that what men profess to be their standards may be denied by their conduct, the existence of common standards makes it more possible for a nation to examine the acts of others to determine whether they are in accord with the common standards. Violators can then be treated accordingly.

For many years the international community shared similar views on how war was to be conducted. A declaration of war was issued. There were common understandings about how prisoners of war were to be treated, how spies were to be dealt with, and how combatants and noncombatants related to each other in war. There were agreements on the use of the high seas, contraband, and the shipping of materials by neutrals to the powers at war. This has changed.

In our world the Marxist nations and the democratic powers entertain different standards. The powers who make up NATO honor the principles which spring from the Judeo-Christian religion, and particularly from the Ten Commandments. They regard treaties as binding. They pledge to support and to defend each other against external attack. They agree that an attack on one is an attack on all, and are committed to repel an attack under Article 51 of the United Nations Charter. These members are Belgium, Canada, Denmark, France, Iceland, Italy, Luxembourg, the Netherlands, Norway, Portugal, the United Kingdom, Greece, Turkey, West Germany, and the United States. This is not a pacifist organization. The agreement does not discuss the rightness or wrongness of war, nor does it spell out what its attitude should be about the use of nuclear devices, although atomic weaponry is a part of its defense stockpile.

NATO does not allow aggression by its members. It is designed as a defense organization against a known enemy, the Soviet Union. There is little or no likelihood that the nations making up NATO will attack each other or, for that matter that they will attack the Soviet Union. They want peace but realize the need for the use of force when needed to prevent an aggressor from taking them over. No need for NATO would have existed if the Soviet Union functioned as a nation on the basis of the same common standards which prevail among the members of NATO, but Russia does not. The Soviet Union and Communists in general operate from a perspective diametrically opposed to that of NATO.

Absence of Absolutes
Virtually every religion bases its ethical and moral standards on an ultimate reality which leads to absolutes for conduct. Some acts are always wrong; others are always right. In the Judeo-Christian tradition, cheating, stealing, and telling lies are wrong. Integrity, rectitude, honesty, and truthfulness are always right. The Marxists pay no attention to such "absurdities." Their principles derive from a different source. In place of God-given morality Marxism substitutes its own absolute—the absence of moral and ethical absolutes. Nothing is right or wrong in itself.

Since the goal of the Communists is extermination of the bourgeoisie and the victory of the proletariat, anything done to attain this objective is permissible, especially in connection with the Communist doctrine of war. Lenin said in his "Farewell Letter to the Swiss Workers": "We are not pacifists. We are opposed to imperialist wars for the division of spoils among the capitalists, but we have always declared it to be absurd for the revolutionary proletariat to renounce revolutionary wars *that may prove necessary in the interests of socialism.*"

Marxists take great pains to distinguish between "just" and "unjust" wars. "Just" wars, by their definition, are those fought by the Soviet Union and its allies. If the "exploiting class" conducts a war, it is bad; if the "proletariat," it is "holy." Lenin wrote:

> . . . Legitimacy and justice from what point of view? Only from the point of view of the socialist proletariat and its struggle for emancipation. We do not recognize any other point of view. If war is waged by the exploiting class with the object of strengthening its class rule, such a war is a criminal war, and "defencism" in *such* a war is a base betrayal of socialism. If war is waged by the proletariat after it has conquered the bourgeoisie in its own country, and is waged with the object of strengthening and extending socialism, such a war is legitimate and "holy."

Gerhart Niemeyer, who was professor of political science at the University of Notre Dame, commented on the Marxist view of war.

> One must conclude, therefore, that the Communist doctrine both expects and justifies the use of war between the "country of the proletarian dictatorship" and the outside world, even though it hopes for the possibility of a "voluntary" admission of defeat by its opponents. It is quite different, though, with respect to wars between "imperialist" countries themselves. These are wars which the Communists not only do not hope to avoid but which they are directed to foment and instigate.[1]

Niemeyer went on to quote Lenin who said:

> . . . the rule . . . which will, until socialism finally triumphs all over the world, remain a fundamental rule with us, namely, that we must take advantage of the antagonisms and

contradictions between two capitalisms, between two systems of capitalist states, inciting one against the other . . . If we are unable to defeat them both, we must know how to dispose our forces in such a way that they fall out among themselves. . . . But as soon as we are strong enough to defeat capitalism as a whole, we shall immediately take it by the scruff of the neck.[2]

Communist Perspective

Those who seek to eliminate the threat of war must understand Lenin's stance, whose views still represent the thinking of the Soviet Union and its allies. Since wars cannot be fought without armaments, the Marxists, to be consistent, cannot and will not do away with conventional weapons at the very least. And they probably will not do away with nuclear devices unless they are forced to do so or can be convinced that it is to their advantage. If the Marxists agreed to disarmament in principle and in fact, it would run counter to their innumerable statements to the opposite. It would alter their world and life-view which is internally consistent if one agrees with their basic presuppositions. If they abridge their doctrine or ethics of war, the system would be unable to endure. No tangible evidences exist to indicate they will change in this regard. Certainly it is important for the free world to *try* to change the Marxist perspective in order to avoid war, but while this effort is made it would be a great risk for the free world to engage in unilateral disarmament or to operate a defense system so inferior to that of the Soviets that it would be useless.

The Marxists work to promote war among the capitalists so Marxists can watch capitalists destroy themselves or at least impair their effectiveness, and the Marxists wage war against "imperialists" to destroy them. We can see this two-headed policy at work in Latin America where Marxists are encouraging the nationals in every country to fight against the "imperialists." It makes no difference whether the "imperialists" are dictators on the right or democrats who support human rights and seek to redress historic imbalances in the use of land and resources. The revolutionaries work to break down governments, create economic crises, terrorize the people who do not support them, and make extravagant promises that have never been fulfilled in any country where Marxists have gained control.

While these revolutionaries wage war against the existing structures, good or bad, Marxists from within the country and from without assert that efforts by such nations as the United States to keep them from victory are unjust, counterrevolutionary, wicked, and depraved. The war of propaganda is greater in scope and intensity than the war with guns and bullets. The Soviets create a backlash in nations like the United States by encouraging its citizens to march against involvement in countries like El Salvador, to foment disturbances, to attack the leadership of the government, and to condition the Congress to vote against appropriations to support the embattled existing government. With such methods the Soviets make gains because many of the Latin American nations are repressive and conduct themselves in a manner which is contrary to the American tradition at home. Human rights are not always honored, and revolutionary activity forces governments to be even more restrictive and coercive than they would be if there were no Communist penetration, no guerrilla activities, and no terrorism.

The Marxist view of war is only one part of an ethical and moral system which extends to every area of life and deprives its own people of human freedoms. One of the persons most sedulously persecuted by the Soviet Union is Andrei Sakharov, who was seized on a street in Moscow by KGB agents, arrested, and exiled to Gorky where he was unable to make contact with the outside world. Scientific colleagues around the world and Western governments worked for his release, but it was useless. In an underground publication, Sakharov wrote:

> In my case at no time has any judicial body formally accused me of any wrongdoing, and I have never been brought to trial. Having isolated me in Gorky, they stripped me of my constitutional right to a fair trial (if there is any reason to try me at all), the right to defense in court, sanctity of the home,

inviolability of what I think and what I write, the right to unhindered correspondence and uninterrupted telephone conversations, the right to be treated by a doctor of my own choice, the right to rest and to travel outside the city limits, the right to free scientific exchanges and contact with people whom I choose to see, and many other rights guaranteed by the constitution of the USSR to citizens of this country. . . . To date I have been unlawfully removed from Moscow and isolated: I have been subjected to burglary without the use of drugs and subjected to theft with the use of drugs. . . . It has been almost three years now since I was deprived of my right to live at home, and I am kept under guard. This is a time period more than sufficient to conduct an investigation and even to have served a sentence for the violation of many articles of the RSFSR Criminal Code. . . . I appeal to the world community to speak out against my unlawful exile and isolation, against new measures of repression, and ask for defense, both legal and humanitarian. I address this appeal to the Heads of State of those countries that have signed the Helsinki Accords, to public servants and to my colleagues, the scientists.[3]

Shadow Document

Sakharov's statement is revealing. He appeals to his constitutional guarantees, guarantees that he knows are contravened by the Criminal Codes. The constitution is a shadow document, a facade. Freedom of speech is guaranteed only where it does not question the Marxist system. Whoever dares to speak against it displays a bourgeois mindset, and such people end up in mental institutions, jail, or the Gulag. Or they are never heard of again.

Elections are rigged, the judiciary is subordinated to the government, political trials are travesties of justice, and the results are foregone conclusions. Behind the system lies the Security Police, otherwise known as the KGB, which was effectively managed, improved, and hardened by the late leader of the Soviet Union, Yuri Andropov. Democracy as it is understood in the West has little meaning in the Soviet Union. Life is so cheap that the statement made by Trotsky years ago is still operative in today's Marxist world: "As for us, we were never concerned with the Kantian-priestly and vegetarian-Quaker prattle about the sanctity of human life."

The Marxist ethic about liberty is simple enough: "When I am weaker, I ask you for liberty because it is your principle; but when I am stronger, I take it away from you because it is not my principle." There is no liberty for people like Sakharov, who happens to be in the public eye because he is a Nobel Peace winner and an eminent scientist. For every Sakharov there are tens of thousands of unknown people who languish in Siberia or who have already perished under a tyranny greater than the world has ever experienced before.

In *The Communist Manifesto* Marx and Engels reveal some of the ethical standards of the Communists: "Communism abolishes all religion and all morality, instead of constituting them on a new basis; it therefore acts in contradiction to all past historical experience." On women and marriage they wrote: "Bourgeois marriage is in reality a system of wives in common, and thus, at the most, what the Communists might possibly be reproached with is that they desire to introduce, in substitution for a hypocritically concealed, an openly legalized community for women." The ethical and moral posture of communism is different from any system of ethics and morality the world has ever known.

Children are trained and educated along lines determined by the state and with regard only to the interests of the state. Religion is forbidden them. Educational opportunities on the collegiate and graduate level are open only to those aproved by the state. Work opportunities depend on faithfulness to the Communist credo. Nonworkers, looked upon as parasites, are sent to labor camps. Only people who have permits can live in Moscow. Travel is curtailed, and whoever uses public transportation for longer trips must record them on their cards, which enables the KGB to keep track of anyone inclined toward dissidency.

Religious activity is supervised. Churches cannot exist without government approval. Parents are not permitted to teach their children the Christian faith. Baptists who believe in soul liberty and who often meet in contravention of the laws of the land are subjected to all sorts of harassment and imprisonment. Clergymen, whose activities are of special concern to the KGB, are watched, their homes invaded, and their freedom always imperiled. The lack of human freedom is also reflected in the state's attitude toward those who wish to emigrate to another nation. Jews in particular often have been prevented from leaving the Soviet Union. More recently the number allowed to leave declined precipitously. Soviet authorities explain a decline by saying that all who wanted to leave have done so. Jewish sources claim that invitations from relatives in Israel to loved ones in the Soviet Union have been systematically intercepted. Unless invitations are sent in distinctive official envelopes, the Soviet authorities will not accept applications from Jewish families for exit visas. At one time the number of emigrants from Communist East Germany reached so high a total that the Berlin Wall was erected to prevent people from leaving. If the Berlin Wall came down tomorrow, the departures from East Germany would rival the flow of immigrants from Europe to the United States in the early twentieth century. Citizens of all the nations in the West are allowed to emigrate.

Reinhold Niebuhr, who was a professor of ethics at Union Seminary in New York, wrote about democracy and communism in two articles which were featured in *The Wall Street Journal* in 1961. He exposed the multiple threat of communism in these words:

> That evil is a pretentious scheme of world salvation, a secularized religious apocalypse, which foolishly divides the world between good and evil classes and nations, predicts the final triumph of the hosts of justice against those of injustice, and destines one class, the "proletariat," to become the masters of the whole historic process, by taking "the leap from the realm of necessity to the realm of freedom."
>
> If this absurd religious apocalypse should ever be implemented on a large scale, and should master the destinies of all the nations, mankind would face not only totalitarian government, but a dangerous effort to press all the vitalities

and forces, the hopes and aspirations of many nations into the restrictive and confining pattern of its scheme of world salvation. The Communist danger is, in short, much more grievous and perilous than we assume it to be if we define it merely as despotism. . . . Communist dictatorship . . . is but the product and instrument of a religio-political dogmatic system with a fantastic ambition to master all the variegated processes of history and press all its themes into one mold, and which promises redemption from all social evil.

Communist Theory and Practice

Reinhold Niebuhr was looking at the Soviet Union from the standpoint of an ethicist. His analysis was based on his perception that Communist theory and practice are indissolubly tied to an ethical system which is contrary to that for which the West has stood for centuries. There can be no peace in the world until one or the other system of ethics wins the day. Emil Brunner, another well-known theologian from Europe, wrote an article in 1961. It serves to alert the West that whatever was true then is still true today, except that the danger has heightened and the international situation is far worse than one could have imagined in 1961. Dr. Brunner wrote much the same thing that Solzhenitsyn is saying now. In part Brunner said:

> The question, "and if communism should be victorious?" is not just an academic one, but rather, in the light of the latest happenings, an all too real one. The question is not meant to frighten, but to awaken. . . . The tactics of communism, contrary to its strategy and its unshakably established goal, are completely mobile, however centrally guided and synchronized. . . . The United States is made to appear, even in Japan, as the primary enemy of mankind, as the imperialist aggressor and as the disturber of the peace of the world. All this in spite of the fact that clearly the only really aggressive imperialism is that of Russia and Red China, an imperialism which rules and exploits the peoples of the world, accomplishing this by brute force. . . . Among the intellectuals (in the U.S.), the feelings of the alleged cultural inferiority of the American people—who supposedly know only the value of the dollar—is disparagingly stressed. Europe's will to defend

itself is being paralyzed through the spread of terror of the atom bomb, which is being yoked simultaneously with a fraudulent peace program, and by impressing all nations with Soviet Russia's successes in the conquest of space. Most alarming is the success Communists have gained in World Protestantism. . . . The opinion became widespread that anti-communism is a sterile position unworthy of a Christian and that one has to "remain in communication with communism." Moscow's peace propaganda was accepted inasmuch as the Church has to, of course, be "for peace." With great passion it accepted and made its own the "fear" of the atom catastrophe, which Moscow propaganda is constantly spreading. This was done by falling for the Communist trick of equating nuclear armament with willingness to wage an atomic war and making the West responsible for it. All this without noticing how Moscow alternately wavered between threats of rockets and Russian superiority in atomic weapons, and the waving of the palm of peace. . . . Whoever warned against unilateral nuclear disarmament, as Bishop Dibelius did, was pointed out as an enemy of Jesus Christ. It was made a cornerstone of supposed Christian thinking that West Germany or Western Europe should be neutralized. . . .

Communism possesses completely—thereby differing from all former tyranny. It completely monopolizes all the means of forming a man. It has the complete propaganda apparatus at its disposal from Kindergarten to University. It controls newspapers, movies, radio and television. It has built up the psychological technique of forming mind and soul in the most cunning ways. It is able to neutralize and destroy, in a most telling way, all influences which are contrary to its goals. The man it creates is a human being minus all that is human, a man without spontaneity or freedom of thought, a man completely part and parcel of the system—this system of consequent atheism. This collective being that has no heart, that has no feeling or conscience, because all that is despised as being bourgeois; this being is the perfect robot of the Socialist state. Done away with are all traces of Christianity and all the means by which Christianity is spread and can remain in existence. . . .

Because the people of the West still live in a world

where thinking for oneself and expressing these thoughts are a matter of course, they are quite incapable of imagining a generation of humanity so completely inhuman. For this reason, they still permit themselves to defame anti-communism as willful, inhuman and unchristian and even indulge in the luxury of fighting anti-communism. It is indeed high time to awake from this madness and to rise up so that we may protect mankind, ourselves, our children and our grandchildren from this ghastly end which will nullify the fruits of all history of man.

All that one can mention in favor of communism—the raising of the standard of living, the increase in the spread of education, the progress in health and hygiene—can never, even if true, make up for the loss of the soul. The extinguishing of the free spirit and man's soul is too high a price to pay. This must be the common creed of all Christians, all religions, and all who believe in the soul of man.[4]

Communist Threat

We have seen the nature of the enemy, that Communist principles ethically are antithetical to those of the West, and we are aware of their intentions. The West shows no disposition to solve the Marxist problem by war; the Soviet Union shows no disposition to change its world and life-view or to abdicate its ethical stance. We are left with the questions: What shall we do to make certain that communism does not succeed in its struggle for world domination? How can we deal with a movement whose leaders we cannot trust, whose views we cannot accept, and whose intentions to destroy us are constantly reiterated?

Knowing that the enemy is implacable, determined, resourceful, and unethical is important when we decide *how* we should combat the Communist threat. We can have no illusions about Soviet intentions and how they move ahead to accomplish their objectives. It is apparent that many different voices in the West are pressing viewpoints that cannot easily be reconciled with other viewpoints. Some suggest action that would lead to the victory of communism over the free world. Other suggestions are more complicated. The more discussion there is and the more the facts are made clear, the easier it will be to foresee the consequences if certain "solutions" were to be adopted. Given the nature of man and the uncertainty of what events might arise to which we have not given thought, it is clear that the possibility of reaching a satisfactory rapprochement with the Soviet Union will not be attained in the immediate future. Should we not, then, examine the various options we have and make prudent decisions as to which one we should choose in the light of our own moral and ethical principles?

8

Pacifism

Pacifism or nonresistance, one of the options before us, is gaining popularity among some of the peoples of the West. Some scholars and savants, idealists, students, and mothers and fathers have opted for pacifism. Pacifism has existed as a choice for centuries. Quakers, Mennonites, and Schwenkfelders, among those who profess the Christian faith, have long supported a pacifist position based on what they think the Bible teaches. Before World War II the Oxford Unionists, most of whom were university students, proclaimed that they would not fight for king or for country. Since then pacifists have included such notables as Albert Einstein, Bertrand Russell, and Robert M. Hutchins. Today many young Americans refuse to register for a draft which has not been called up and which good people hope will never be called up. Thousands have taken to the streets in favor of pacifism, and a significant number of books have been published both by Christians and non-Christians. Jonathan Schell, who is surely not connected with the Christian faith, has written a popular book, *The Fate of the Earth,* to which we have referred in connection with the impact it made in the mind of Professor Kaufman of Harvard Divinity School. Ronald Sider and Richard K. Taylor have coauthored a book, *Nuclear Holocaust and Christian Faith.* Written by men within the evangelical tradition of Christianity, it contains an earnest plea for the pacifist stance and offers an action-program *vis a vis* resisting the imperial march of the Soviet Union.

Minority View

Sider and Taylor agree that pacifism is a minority opinion. They write: "A minority have believed that Christians ought never to participate in lethal violence. The majority have assumed a 'just war' stance, asserting that although war is always horrible it may sometimes be the lesser of two evils."[1]

They come down much stronger on the question of nuclear war. To this end they offer the support of a number of influential evangelicals who do not accept the pacifist position per se but who are or who may appear to be pacifistic with respect to nuclear armaments and their use. John R. W. Stott of England has said: "Every Christian, whatever he may think of the possibility of a 'just use' of conventional weapons, must be a nuclear pacifist."[2] Billy Graham said:

> The present arms race is a terrifying thing, and it is almost impossible to overestimate its potential for disaster. . . . Is a nuclear holocaust inevitable if the arms race is not stopped? Frankly, the answer is almost certainly yes. . . . I cannot see any way in which nuclear war could be branded as being God's will. Such warfare, if it ever happens, will come because of the greed and pride and covetousness of the human heart.[3]

The authors of *Nuclear Holocaust and Christian Faith* also name some of the evangelical Christians who signed their names to the 1978 statement "A Call to Faithfulness," which was composed by a group of Roman Catholic and Protestant scholars. In part it said:

> Our primary allegiance to Jesus Christ and his kingdom commits us to total abolition of nuclear weapons. There can be no qualifying or conditioning used. We, the signers of this declaration, commit ourselves to non-cooperation with our country's preparation for nuclear war. On all levels—research, development, testing, production, deployment and actual use of nuclear weapons—we commit ourselves to resist in the name of Jesus.

The authors continued, "More surprising perhaps was the large number of prominent evangelical signers: Joseph Bayly of David C. Cook; Ted W. Engstrom of World Vision; Jay Kesler, president of Youth for Christ; theologian Clark Pinnock; Richard Halverson, now chaplain of the U.S. Senate; Frank Gaebelein, former co-editor of *Christianity Today;* and Vernon Grounds of the Conservative Baptist Theological Seminary in Denver."[4] Not mentioned is a longer list of prominent evangelicals who did not sign the statement.

Authors Sider and Taylor also enlist Jim Wallis, editor of *Sojourners* magazine who wrote:

> The sign of the nuclear age is the Bomb. The sign of Christ is the Cross. The Bomb is the countersign to the Cross; it arrogantly threatens to undo the work that the Cross has done. In the Cross, all things are reconciled; in the Bomb, all things are destroyed. In the Cross, violence is defeated; in the Bomb violence is victorious. In the Cross, evil has been overcome; in the Bomb, evil has dominion. In the Cross, death is swallowed up; in the Bomb, death reigns supreme. Which will hold sway in our time?[5]

Mr. Wallis' language is extravagant in that nothing will at last be victorious over the cross of Jesus Christ. God has dominion over all creation and will not allow himself to be defeated. Man proposes, but God disposes.

Pacifism and Jesus

The authors of the book cite the person and teaching of Jesus as a basis for their pacifist stance, but it is questionable whether the Scripture they use supports this viewpoint. They appear not to have taken into account that Jesus as a member of the Trinity participated in the commands of God to destroy certain nations as recorded in the Old Testament. Jesus cannot be considered an advocate of pacifism unless this is resolved.

Authors Sider and Taylor make a sincere effort to deal with the incident in which Jesus cleansed the temple, but in doing so they appear to have contradicted themselves by what they say.

Nor was Jesus nonresistant when he cleansed the temple, driving the animals out with a whip, dumping the money tables upside down and denouncing the moneychangers as robbers. If Matthew 5:39 means that all forms of resistance to evil are forbidden, then Jesus contradicted his own teaching. Jesus certainly did not kill the moneychangers. Indeed we doubt that he even used his whip on them. But he carefully resisted their evil in a dramatic act of nonviolent resistance.[6]

In the accounts by Mark and Luke we read, "He began to drive out those who sold and those who bought in the temple" (Mark 11:15; Luke 19:45), and in Matthew, "Jesus drove out all who sold and bought in the temple" (21:12). The same Greek word is used in connection with Jesus casting out demons and implies power or force. We may grant that Jesus did not use whips on them. We may agree that what he did was accomplished by his word, but who can suppose that they would have obeyed his word if they did not sense the force or power which lay in what he said? The Scripture also says that he overturned the tables of the moneychangers and the seats of those who sold pigeons. That was a violent action. Perhaps it can be argued that the force was applied to tables, animals, and seats. In that event it was force used as a deterrent so that he did not need to use force on the people involved. The deterrence was sufficient. It appears inconsistent to say that Jesus used nonviolent resistance when the "dramatic act" involved the use of force.

Since it is apparent that Jesus used force, can we agree with authors Sider and Taylor that if such was the case, then Jesus "contradicted his own teaching"? Response to this possibility is that Matthew 5:39 refers to person-to-person relationships and does not apply to structured evil or national evil.

Nonviolent Restraints

They also write about the use of police power. "Our view in no way advocates anarchy. It does not require that we abolish the police or the law courts. Rather it suggests that police ought to develop nonviolent ways to restrain criminals and that the law courts should apply disciplinary rather than retributive punishment."[7] They do not say how it would be possible "to develop nonviolent ways to restrain criminals," especially if lawbreakers have guns and use them against the police who, under this proposal, would not be able to fire back. And how would the police stop such crimes if they were unarmed and could not use physical force? It is difficult to see how a lawbreaker who resisted could be put behind bars if no force is used.

These men are no Communists; they regard communism as an evil. They say we must resist aggression. The question is, how do they propose we resist the evil? They allege that Christianity can survive under the worst conditions and reproduce itself. While this is assuredly true, it does not follow that men should peacefully allow the Communists to take them over.

The authors propose a civilian-based defense system (CBD). "During the several-year process of preparing for CBD, we would get rid of all nuclear and conventional weapons."[8] This is unilateral disarmament covering nuclear and conventional weaponry. They continue realistically, "We believe that such an action could very likely result in a Soviet invasion." Such a takeover by the Soviets is not only likely; it is certain to take place. And it could be done without armed invasion tactics. Since no one would lay a hand on a Soviet citizen, there would be no need for armament. The authors, assuming there would be a military landing, make this recommendation:

> The landing would be peaceful. No American artillery would fire; no jets would strafe. Instead of American soldiers crouching behind tanks and pointing guns at them, the invaders would see thousands of unarmed people carrying signs with messages in the invader's language: Go Home! We Won't Harm You; Don't Shoot—We Are Your Brothers and Sisters; Your Life is Precious; You Are a Child of God.[9]

The first serious problem has to do with basic theology in their referring to the invaders as children of God. The Bible distinguishes between those who by reason of the new birth or regeneration are the children of God and those who are not.

Paul says, "So through God you are no longer a slave but a son, and if a son then an heir" (Galatians 4:7). Jesus said to some Jews, "You are of your father the devil, and your will is to do your father's desires" (John 8:44). Unbelievers are not children of God. They are children of the devil unless and until they exercise faith in Jesus Christ as their Savior. The supposition that unbelieving Soviets are children of God has devastating implications.

Freedom Lost
The second problem is one which is already validated by the experience of nations which have come under the control of Soviet communism. Human freedom and human rights are lost immediately. The peoples of any subjugated nation become slaves. Lech Walesa of Poland is a witness to this fact. A winner of the Nobel Peace Prize, he has sought to deliver his country from the yoke of communism by peaceful resistance. His testimony includes an appeal to America to end sanctions against his nation. There is an economic crisis "with dramatic consequences for the very existence of Polish families." Yet the Soviet-controlled government of Poland insists that it will not talk to Solidarity, the agency of peaceful resistance to communism.[10]

Poland no longer produces enough food to feed the nation, whereas it formerly exported food. This is a direct result of the Communist takeover. Wherever the Socialists assume power, economic conditions plummet and people face starvation. The first thing the Soviets would do would be to strip America of its wealth. They would take everything movable and send it to the Soviet Union to improve their own economy. They would seize all the grain for Soviet consumption. The Soviet Union would control industry, transportation, the media, the banks, and the farms. America would be helpless. Whoever did not toe the Soviet line would be shot or sentenced to a prison or gulag. Compassion is an unknown characteristic among Communists. Although the authors do not recommend cooperation with the enemy, they call for peaceful resistance; either way the end of the line is utterly disastrous. A certain irony is seen in Dr. Sider's position. He has spent time and energy in appeals to feed the poor, lift up the downtrodden, and reverse injustice; but his position would bring the greatest injustice possible, and it would end all possibility for America to do anything to feed the poor and promote justice. America itself would be poor and in need of help from other compassionate nations.

Pacifism would constitute an ideal weapon for the Communists. The Soviets do not wish war unless force is required to attain their objectives. Rather, the Soviets prefer to take over a nation by peaceful means, and they have devised programs calculated to breed fear so as to produce a malaise which will strangle all notions of armed defense. We have evidences which demonstrate that the peace movement in the United States is orchestrated in many ways by the Communists. They are spending huge sums of money to infiltrate, direct, and use pacifism to accomplish the overthrow of the American system. At least Dr. Sider's pacifism is based on the belief that this is the will of God for men and nations. Far more people are pacifists simply because they are frightened and terrorized by the thought of death.

Consequences of Pacifism

Regardless of the reason for accepting pacifism, it should be clear that those who take this position are helping the enemy to gain his objective. And must not those who assist wicked men and nations face the moral and ethical consequences which flow from this fact? Given the nature of the aggressor, pacifism does nothing to stop the assault. Does it not actually encourage aggression? It is one of the hard lessons of history that evil men will always take advantage of those who sit by and do nothing to prevent aggression. Can a pacifist think of himself as guiltless when his nonresistance leads either to slavery or death?

We can suppose a senario in which the Soviets land in Washington and go to the White House and the halls of Congress to take over the government. The pacifists do nothing except protest verbally that the enemy should not do this. They can lie down on the carpets of the White House and sit on the marble floors of the Capitol building, but the peaceful protesters will be ordered to depart. If they are pacifists because they would rather be enslaved than dead, they will quickly learn to obey the orders of the new masters, because the Soviets would not fail to use force to make their victims do exactly what they want them to do. Thus, even by peaceful programs pacifists will invite the force which they themselves have disavowed. Does not making the enemy use force to accomplish his purpose raise still another moral dilemma? If I by my actions make it necessary for someone else to use force which I have disavowed, am I not in some measure guilty when this takes place?

The Christian pacifist thinks he is doing the will of God. He is willing to lay down his life for his principle; yet it is a principle that has never commended itself to substantial majorities who have understood the Bible differently. Certainly a majority vote constitutes no ground for assuming that it is the voice of God. Majorities have been wrong in bygone days and minorities have sometimes been right, but minorities should be careful not to presume they are right when the verdict of church history is against them.

Like the non-Christian pacifist, the Christian advocate of pacifism is also an accessory because his position is an open invitation to aggressors to act. He becomes a participant by his refusal to defend himself and his nation. Since he does not accept the notion that it is better to be enslaved, he runs into the moral problem of committing suicide. No Christian pacifist is likely to do that, at least not at first; but suicide by another's hand is another side of the coin. The Christian pacifist knowingly forces the hand of the Communist aggressor to kill him unless he becomes a proletarian. If he becomes a proletarian, he must demit the Christian faith, for this class entertains a world and life-view that rests on an atheist base. And this the Christian pacifist cannot accept. By failing to resist the Communist aggressor by more than peaceful means, he guarantees his own suicide.

Suicide is not a biblical option; but capital punishment for those who spurn and disobey the laws of God is. The Communist who would kill the pacifist has by that intention forfeited his right to life. He who kills the aggressor who would take the *imago dei* from him is not guilty of murder. Is not the Christian who fights and kills to preserve his own life and to protect the *imago dei* in himself in a far stronger position than the pacifist who by his pacifism encourages the Communist to kill him and to erase the *imago dei* in him?

By refusing to repel the aggressor, the pacifists have averted war in a technical sense; but once the aggressor takes over, it is now possible to reconstitute the political and social structures according to the enemy's world and life-view. We can be sure that the newly imposed constitution would be no different from that which governs Soviet society today. The pacifist has won the day by keeping the nation from war. The price, however, has implications for the Christian faith and its world and life-view.

Biblically, the first and greatest of all human rights is the freedom to worship God according to the dictates of the human conscience. This is a far-ranging freedom, for it guarantees to the atheist the right to disbelieve even as it assures me that I have the right to believe. All of my other human rights spring from my freedom of religion. These rights include the freedom of speech even when it disagrees with the prevailing system. It includes the right to disseminate my views through books, radio, and television. I am free to live where I please, to engage in whatever occupation appeals to me, and to move from one location to another. It also includes the right for me to leave the country of my birth, to relocate in another country, and to take an oath of allegiance to the new country in which I choose to reside.

The Pacifist and Human Rights

In Communist countries none of these rights exist in any meaningful sense. The pacifist by his refusal to wage war to retain his basic human rights is sure to lose them. The pacifism which made Communist victory possible will be denied to him under the new regime. He will no longer be permitted to be a pacifist, nor will he have the freedom to dissent or to propagate his viewpoint. The irony is that the success of pacifism guarantees its end.

The Soviet understanding of the freedom of speech is the opposite of what it means to us in the Western world. Whoever fails to grasp this fact is living under an illusion. Any departure from what the ruling class defines as proper thought is taboo and does not fall under the rubric of freedom of speech.

The activities of the pacifists today consist almost entirely in efforts having to do with international relationships. They apparently do not see that their inability to do in any single nation what they want done in the arena of international relations is intrinsically contradictory. If parts of the world cannot function within the guidelines laid down by the pacifists, how can these guidelines work effectively in the international scene?

Pacifism has not yet worked in the United States. Here the pacifists have the most congenial atmosphere to prove their case. They have not done so, and the possibility of their doing it appears very remote. Each year more laws are added to the statute books because more than ever before people are doing things they should not do. The laws of the nation are intended to support nonviolence and oppose the use of force by the citizens, but in doing so it becomes necessary for the government to use force to control wrong actions of individuals.

It is a crime for someone to assault me, to steal my property including my ideas, to keep my factory from functioning, or to prevent me from earning a living at my job. None of these laws would be necessary if all people did what is right, but not all people do what is right. Wrongdoing has existed at all times and in all cultures and will continue to exist unless and until all people can be made good. There is nothing by way of evidence to show that all people will soon become good. Moreover, for the Christian there is a sure word from God that the Paradise which was lost by Adam in Eden will not be regained until Jesus Christ comes. Only after Satan and sin have been dealt with will the utopia we all yearn for become a reality.

Pacifism is utopian. It offers a hope that cannot be fulfilled by man. It fails to take seriously the nature of man, the existence of sin, and the unremitting diligence with which people generally violate the best of laws which are designed to produce peace and safety. In the long run, when the illusions created by pacifism have evaporated, the people most influenced by it are likely to become disenchanted, cynical, and unconcerned to work for realistic possibilities by which peace can be maintained. Intrinsic to this viewpoint, even though unstated, is the refusal to believe that the Soviet mentality can be as despotic, degenerate, and as immoral as its critics assert and for which they can produce almost limitless evidence.

In the meantime the Soviet Union and other Communist countries paint an idyllic picture of what life is like under socialism. So effective is this propaganda that many innocent and naive people come to believe that whoever fights against the Communist menace in Latin America and elsewhere is heartless, guilty of repression, an imperialist, and an opponent of the masses. Experts in psychological warfare, the Soviets seek to brainwash the people of the West into believing that the greatest of all evils is capitalism. The leadership of some of America's religious bodies have fallen for this bait. Given an imperfect world and sinful people, no one should suppose that capitalism does not suffer from the effects of men's sins; but when one weighs the evils of socialism over against those of capitalism it can readily be seen that capitalism is far and away the better of the two systems.

Worthy Objectives
All of this should not, however, keep us from appreciating the major objective of true pacifists who are not Communists and do not play the Communist game, and who frequently are members of pacifist Christian denominations. They want to prevent war, which they think to be evil in itself. In this effort they should be joined by other Christians who think there is a need for police power and who hold that there are just as well as unjust wars. We should try to prevent war. We should do all in our power to defuse the nuclear holocaust threat. On this there can be general agreement. Once we have said this, there is the more difficult question which comes to haunt us and to keep open the avenues of discussion—what are the best means by which we can prevent wars of any kind?

So far as the Soviet Union is concerned, pacifism would

prevent a nuclear war. It would not be needed, for the Communists would win without firing a shot. It would also inevitably lead to the loss of freedom and yield as its final product a slavery the world has not seen until the emergence of communism in this century.

Yuri V. Andropov, who was the top man in the Communist hierarchy and was once the head of the dreaded KGB, said: "Revolution is destructive [but] without destruction it is impossible to create a new Socialist world." V. I. Lenin said in a report to the VII Congress of the Russian Communist Party, on March 8, 1918: "Marxists have never forgotten that violence is the inevitable accomplishment to the collapse of capitalism on its fullest scale and of the birth of a Socialist country." Lenin further said: "In principle we have never rejected, nor can we reject, terror. Terror is one of the forms of military action that may be perfectly suitable, even essential, at a definite junction in the struggle." In 1977 Communist Party Secretary Boris N. Ponomarev said: "Violence in itself is not an evil. It depends on what its purpose is. In the hands of Socialists, it is a progressive force." In connection with the rape of Afghanistan, Yuri V. Andropov said: "Our response to events in Afghanistan was a lofty act of loyalty to the principle of proletarian internationalism, which was necessary to defend the interest of Motherland." *The Soviet Military Encyclopedia* says: "The change in the correlation of forces in the international arena in favor of socialism has led to the activization of the struggle by the peoples of Latin American . . . which opens the way to Socialism in the Western Hemisphere."[11]

In *The Philosophical Heritage of V. I. Lenin and Problems of Contemporary War* (1972), edited in part by General-Major A. S. Milovidov, the statement is made that "Nuclear War has not ceased to be an instrument of politics, as is claimed by the overwhelming majority of the representatives of pacifist, anti-war movements in the bourgeois world." And as early as 1928 a Resolution of the VI World Congress of the Communist International said, "The international policy of the USSR is a peace policy. . . . it is merely another—under present conditions—more advantageous form of fighting capitalism." And finally in 1980 in *Questions of Philosophy,* General-Major A. S. Milovidov and Dr. Ye A. Zhdanov said: "Marxist-Leninists decisively reject the assertions of certain bourgeois theoreticians who consider nuclear missile war unjust from any point of view."[12]

Whoever decides in favor of pacifism must first understand what the Soviet Union is and what it stands for. Against this backdrop the quest for peace and the prevention of war through the pacifist position appears unsatisfactory.

The United States fought the Civil War to end slavery. If the South had been pacifist, the slavery problem could have been settled without recourse to war. The rightness of those who wanted to abolish slavery cannot be denied. The means to abolish slavery could have been something other than war. But once the South refused to settle the problem apart from force of arms, the North had only two possible choices: permit slavery to continue, or fight to abolish it. To permit slavery to continue would have been a greater evil than to fight to abolish it. Since the Bible does not prohibit a just war, there could be no moral right to allow the continuation of the South's "peculiar institution."

Pacifism in the face of the Communist threat would be capitulation to an evil far greater than anything represented by the Civil War in the United States. Just as the Civil War could have been averted, so it is possible that nuclear and other war can be averted, but not by pacifism.

9

Unilateral Disarmament

When we speak about unilateral disarmament we must first consider the possibility of bilateral disarmament, by which we mean that both the Soviet Union and the United States would disarm completely. For the Soviet Union to disarm would run counter to its basic philosophy. In the works of Marx, Engels, Lenin, Stalin, Krushchev, Brezhnev, or Andropov, the use of force is a common theme. Force is the midwife which will lead to the extermination of the bourgeoisie. Force may consist simply in threats designed to bring about the surrender of the non-Marxist nations. The existence of nuclear weaponry in itself poses the threat of force. Or it may take a more overt form through the use of terrorism. Any of these creates a climate of fear to convince peoples and nations of the hopelessness of resistance and to bring them to a place of giving in to the demands of the Marxists.

Conventional military power poses a threat also, as we see in Poland where the people are held in check by Communist Polish soldiers and where Soviet troops ring that unhappy land. The smaller nations such as Hungary, Czechoslovakia, Romania, Finland, and Latvia are incapable of resisting Soviet domination because of the Soviets' military might which will be used if necessary to "pacify" these conquered peoples. The invasion of Afghanistan by conventional military means shows that the Soviets will employ actual force when its suits their purposes. No thoughtful observer could conclude that Afghanistan is a threat to the Soviet Union. It is, however, a barrier to the designs of the Soviets in their onward movement to attain world conquest. One look at the map of that area shows that Afghanistan is contiguous to Iran and is an important component in connection with oil and the Middle East. The Soviets wish to control that region for two purposes: to guarantee sufficient oil supplies for any contingency, and to control the sale and distribution of Middle Eastern oil to non-Communist nations.

The grand design of the Soviets includes control of southern Africa and the seaways around the tip of that continent. They also want to control the sea-lanes in the Caribbean region so as to prevent oil from coming to the United States if and when that is necessary. Few Americans are aware of the strategic implications of the Caribbean control problem, nor do they understand the military significance of Grenada with regard to the passage of oil from the Middle East.

The second reason why the Soviet Union is unlikely to agree to bilateral disarmament involves the consequences that would result from such action. Poland would immediately be free to throw out its Communist masters. Other nations behind the Iron Curtain would rise up overnight, for the Soviets would have no means to control them. Disarmament would have internal consequences as well. The people of the Soviet Union would be free to open the prison doors of the incarcerated; Sakharov would be free to return to Moscow. The media would be reduced to ruins. The farmers would reclaim their lost lands. Individual enterprise would be reestablished. In short, communism would be dead. Even if we were to suppose, as some do, that the present leaders of the Soviet Union no longer believe the basic teachings of Marxism, it would make no difference. They are confirmed dictators who show no willingness to abdicate their present control of this great empire. It is unrealistic to expect the Soviets to agree to bilateral disarmament. No nation created and sustained by force is likely to commit voluntary suicide.

Moral or Strategic?

Since it is unrealistic to expect the Soviets to disarm in the bilateral sense, what about unilateral disarmament on the part of the United States? First we must ask, Is unilateral disarmament based on strategy or on moral principle? If it is based on moral principle, then it can only mean that the possession and use of armaments are for one reason or another immoral. If this principle cannot be sustained on the basis of the Judeo-Christian tradition, it has no foundation on which to rest. It becomes someone's opinion and has binding force only as it appeals to other people. It has no transcendent significance and at best can be only utilitarian. If it is based on the morality of the Judeo-Christian tradition, it faces the obstacles we have already mentioned—that God himself in the Old Testament ordered the use of armed force, and the Israelites employed it as a protective measure when they returned from the captivity to rebuild the walls of Jerusalem.

If unilateral disarmament is based on strategic considerations, it is a matter of prudence, expediency, and the hope that it will be a method by which nuclear and even conventional war can be avoided. The concept of unilateral disarmament carries with it the implied idea that those who endorse this approach will not use any kind of forceful resistance against invaders. The most it offers is the hope that such a policy will persuade the Communists to abandon their aggressive expansionism and constrain them from taking over the United States at will. However advocates of unilateral disarmament state the case, it amounts to voluntary surrender. On the basis of the historical evidence, the Soviets would be delighted with unilateral disarmament by the United States and would move in to take control over us. Any efforts of a peaceful sort to resist such a takeover or to prevent the Soviets from continuing their supremacy would be met by force. The United States would become another Poland.

Another explicit or implied judgment connected with unilateral disarmament is manifested among those who are not pacifists and would not accept the pacifist approach. It is a matter of expediency based on the notion that living is preferable to dying. Hosts of people, however, believe that this life is not the *summum bonum* of all things. They do not think the Bible teaches that *any* alternative is better than death. They think that life under the yoke of communism is a worse state of affairs than death itself—it is a living death. This is supported by the teaching of the Bible that death is the doorway to eternal life and that life's ultimate goal is reunion with Jesus Christ in a transcendental sense. All of us must face these facts and make a choice, but expediency in making a choice can never be the determining factor unless there are sufficient biblical data to show that it is simply a matter of expediency and not of principle.

Idolatry of Our Age?
The argument favoring unilateral disarmament has in it still another implication of special interest to those in the Judeo-Christian tradition. Substantively some believe that any dependence on military power is a denial of the sovereignty of God to protect his people and nations. Those who favor armaments (and this, of course, means not simply nuclear armaments, but conventional ones as well) are not trusting in God to deliver them. Such is the view articulated by thoughtful Christians like Gordon Cosby, the pastor of the Church of the Saviour in Washington, D.C. In a brochure which is a reprint of an article published by the *Sojourners* magazine and World Peacemakers he urges Christians to "focus on true security in a world threatened by the nuclear arms race." He says that in the case of nuclear missiles, if we trusted God "we would be safer without them." The same argument can be made about conventional arms. He holds that "the issue of national security . . . is the overriding idolatry of our age," that "the accumulation of nuclear arms is contrary to what it means to trust God and to believe that he will act in our behalf as he acted again and again in Israel's history." His case is complete when he writes, "I want to focus on a particular idolatry which makes a mockery of the so-called faith of millions of Christians: our dependence on military expenditures for 'national defense.' This state of affairs is a negation of biblical faith."

Using a biblical incident to bulwark his thesis, Dr. Cosby mentions Moses, "our liberator, [who] went stuttering into the presence of Pharaoh with a rod in his hand. It was God who acted, who brought his people safely across on dry land."

Those of us who uphold the doctrine of the sovereignty of God in the affairs of men must take Dr. Cosby's statement to heart. It would appear that we are inconsistent if we accept the notion of a just war fought by men instead of trusting in God to deliver us without resorting to secondary means. What biblical response can we make to this stand of Dr. Cosby? It is plain, to be sure, that Dr. Cosby is asking for unilateral disarmament and for ceasing to spend money for national defense. He is also claiming that it is wrong "to take the major share of the world's resources from the daily needs of people and use them to make credible our threat to commit mass murder."

Either/Or Question?

Is it an either/or or a both/and problem? Dr. Cosby makes it an either/or question. If we build a nuclear stockpile, we are not trusting God. We must choose between trusting in God or trusting in armaments. The other possibility is that we can trust God and also surround ourselves with armaments. Is doing this an indication that we do not trust God? Dr. Cosby says yes. Other Christians say no. No Christians are saying that we should trust our armaments and not trust God. But they do not agree with Dr. Cosby that spending money on armaments necessarily means a lack of faith in God.

In the development of his thesis, Dr. Cosby suggests that a binding principle comes from the example of Moses, who faced Pharaoh with nothing but a rod in his hands. He had neither soldiers nor armaments. What Dr. Cosby fails to make clear is the fact that the children of Israel had no other choice. There was no way they could develop an army or manufacture armaments to aid them in their struggle against Pharaoh. A sovereign God knew this and arranged for Israel's deliverance in a supernatural way. However, we must not forget that in doing so, God slew many of the Egyptians as he closed the waters of the Red Sea over them. This was force, and it was war. Should we stop at this point and lay down the premise that it is the will of God for his people never to use force or to accumulate weapons of warfare; rather, they are always to look to God for deliverance without recourse to human or secondary means?

In Exodus we read that the children of Israel en route to the Promised Land encountered the Amalekites. This pagan nation "fought with Israel at Rephidim" (17:8). Then we read that Moses said to Joshua, "Choose us men, and go out, fight with Amalek; tomorrow I will stand on the top of the hill with the rod of God in my hand" (17:9). Is it not significant that this was the same rod that Moses used when he faced Pharaoh? Only this time he used it in connection with armed might as the warriors of Israel used force against the Amalekites. God told Moses: "I will utterly blot out the remembrance of Amalek from under heaven" (17:14). Why didn't Moses trust God for deliverance from the Amalekites without the use of armed force? Was his use of armed force an indication that he did not trust God? His use of armed force had divine approval. Moses did what Dr. Cosby opposes in our day.

In today's world there are peoples whose condition is similar to that of the Israelites in Egypt. They have no means to find deliverance from their oppression by the Soviet Union based on force. They are shut up to the necessity for divine miraculous deliverance. Other nations, however, have the money and the ability to resist aggression through armed means. Should they then disarm and open themselves to the same fate as the captive nations? A no to this question does not imply that a Christian should favor either war or the use of nuclear military power per se. Universal disarmament and the peaceful defusing and abandonment of all nuclear weapons and conventional ones as well is a high and desirable priority. But unilateral disarmament by the United States does not appear to be the best or even a possible way to accomplish this objective. Rather, it opens the door to more frightening possibilities not only for the United States, but for the people of the whole world, including the oppressed peoples in the Soviet Union.

A number of advocates of pacifism and of unilateral disarmament spread quotations from Billy Graham over their pages to support views that Dr. Graham does not entertain. In his latest book, *Approaching Hoofbeats*, Dr. Graham says: "I am *not for unilateral disarmament—and I am not a pacifist.* As long as America's security is threatened—and I am not naive about the intentions of those who radically oppose our way of life and our commitment to freedom—we must have strong defenses."[1]

Dr. Graham's views are quite different from those of Dr. Cosby, *Sojourners*, and *The Other Side*. Does this mean, in the language of Dr. Cosby, that Dr. Graham who advocates strong defense is guilty of "the overriding idolatry of our age"? Does it mean that because Dr. Graham advocates strong defense he does not trust God for deliverance? Surely no Christian leader in America or around the world has a better track record of calling the nations of the world back to God in repentance and faith. And none has done better than he in calling for the end of war and the dismantlement of all nuclear weapons. He does say that pacifism and unilateral disarmament are not good choices to resolve the nuclear dilemma. And by advocating strong defenses he is saying that force may be necessary in a sinful world. He is a realist, not a utopian idealist.

Should Small Nations Disarm?
Any discussion of unilateral disarmament should not be limited to the superpowers. There are smaller nations for whom the question is equally important. Anyone who has traveled in Israel as I have becomes aware of the problem facing the people of Israel. If the Israelis decided to disarm unilaterally, what would the consequences be? In order to answer this question we need to reflect on the Arab-Israeli history of the past half-century. At the turn of the twentieth century the British offered the Zionist Jews 6,000 square miles of Uganda for a national homeland. It was turned down because it was not in Palestine, long regarded by the Jews as their true homeland. After World War I, Palestine became a British-mandated territory. Jews were allowed to return to Palestine. Following World War II the United Nations recognized the independence of Israel as a sovereign nation-state. A number of wars were fought between the Arabs and the Israelis subsequent to independence. The Israelis expanded their possessions and rooted out hundreds of thousands of the Palestinians, who became refugees. Soon Israel was a potent military power in that region, controlling all of Jerusalem and making it the key city of the nation.

From the very beginning of the Jewish presence in Palestine, the Arab nations made it clear that they regarded the Israelis as intruders who must be removed from the land. Surrounded by 100 million Islamic Arabs, the state of Israel is minuscule. Arab leaders such as King Hussein of Jordan have pledged to regain control of the Israeli-occupied lands for the displaced Palestinians. Thus Israel and the Arab world continually confront each other, and no solution satisfactory to both parties is in sight. The situation, *de facto*, is that Israel occupies lands that the Arabs believe to be theirs, even as the Israelis contend that it belongs to them. Israel refuses to surrender lands to the Palestinians, and the Arabs refuse to accept as normative the present state of Israel.

If the Israelis were to disarm unilaterally while the surrounding Arab nations possess military means to invade and overcome the Israelis, the Israelis would either be genocided or displaced. Jerusalem would be lost to them, and they either would roam the face of the earth without a homeland or be forced to live in some sort of ghetto situation. Should they decide to disarm, no nation in the world would come to Israel's side, for the act of disarming would be tacit reason for no one else to employ force when the Israelis themselves had chosen not to.

Invitation to Suicide?

Given the circumstances, unilateral disarmament would be an invitation to suicide for the Israelis, even as unilateral disarmament by the United States in its contest with the Soviet Union would be an act of suicide. No clear mandate from God requires the Israelis to disarm and leave themselves in the hands of God alone without any defense. If there were such a mandate, they should certainly disarm and trust God in the light of Judeo-Christian tradition. It seems appropriate for Israel to arm against the express intention of the enemy to dispossess them from the land. This should not blind us to the inequity accorded the displaced Arabs, but it is strange indeed that other Arab nations with land and money to spare have offered no substantive arrangements to help their Islamic brothers and sisters in the hour of their need.

In the final analysis, unilateral disarmament by the United States would be foolhardy unless and until the Soviet Union alters its basic objectives and commitment. This would include rejection of the teachings of its earlier founding fathers and the leaders who followed them. John Cardinal Krol wrote this about communism:

> Lenin was blunt in saying, "Every religious idea of God, even flirting with the idea of God, is unutterable vileness of the most dangerous kind, contagion of the most abominable kind. Millions of sins, filthy deeds, acts of violence, and physical contagions are far less dangerous than the subtle spiritual idea of God."
>
> Lenin also said, "We must hate, hatred is the basis of communism." He also enunciated a new ethic: "Everything is moral which is necessary for the annihilation of the old exploiting order."
>
> The Communists talk a great deal about peace, but it is important to understand their concept of peace. Lenin gives us an idea of that concept in these words: "After we have totally defeated and expropriated the bourgeoisie throughout the entire world, wars will no longer be possible. The victory of socialism in a country will by no means exclude or eliminate all wars. On the contrary, this victory makes wars inevitable." This is another way of saying that there will be no peace until communism subjugates the entire world, and that detente and coexistence are only periods of rest and regrouping of the forces that must conquer the whole world. . . .
>
> Coexistence of religion and atheistic communism is as impossible as the coexistence of fire and water.[2]

Cardinal Krol also quoted approvingly a statement made by Pope Paul VI in October of 1965, a statement which has been reiterated by the present Pope, John Paul II.

> No more war—war never again. . . . If you want to be brothers, let the weapons fall from your hands. One cannot love with offensive weapons in his hands. . . . As long as man

remains that weak, changeable and even wicked being he often shows himself to be, defensive armaments will, alas, be necessary.[3]

Thus the hierarchy of the Roman Catholic Church joins hands with Protestant believers who entertain a similar viewpoint: unilateral disarmament against the backdrop of what the Soviets believe and practice would itself be immoral behavior. That the Soviets have no intention of disarming is obvious in the late Mr. Brezhnev's remarks that no nation which has embraced socialism shall ever be allowed to reverse itself and turn away from socialism. Force will be applied, he said, to keep any Socialist nation from abdicating its socialism.

Unilateral disarmament is opposed by many who may not stand in the Christian tradition and who are among the most liberal in their thinking. Arthur M. Schlesinger, speech-writer for John Kennedy and author of a book explaining and defending the 1000-day presidency of Kennedy, writes:

> We cannot acquiesce in the drift toward Armageddon. For the stake is supreme: it is the fate of humanity itself. Let me say at once that the answer to the arms race is not unilateral disarmament. The renunciation of nuclear weapons by the West would place the democratic world at the mercy of Soviet Communism. History has proven beyond all argument that mercy is not a salient characteristic of any Communist regime. Neither the arms race nor unilateral disarmament holds out any hope. What we must do is to revive the art of diplomacy.[4]

10

Nuclear Freeze

The pacifist and unilateral disarmament approaches have limitations and implications which make them undesirable to those in the biblical tradition who do not think it is better to submit to communism than to be dead. Nuclear freeze is another possibility to consider. This option has probably received more attention recently than any other suggested solution as the best change to prevent the annihilation of life.

A very substantial worldwide crusade in favor of an immediate nuclear freeze has had for its first priority that the United States should not seek to attain military parity with the Soviet Union. No one looking at the efforts to bring about a nuclear freeze should disagree with the desirability of a freeze on both nuclear and conventional armaments. So appealing is the notion among some leaders in the United States that on March 10, 1982, long before the high tide of demonstrations, Mark Hatfield and Edward Kennedy introduced in the U.S. Senate a resolution calling for an immediate nuclear freeze. A similar resolution was introduced in the House of Representatives. The resolutions did not have the force of law on the United States, and certainly not on the Soviet Union.

Where did the worldwide clamor for a nuclear freeze come from? Is it a natural phenomenon, or is it the result of powerful forces at work to bring it about? Many of the participants are patriotic, concerned individuals who sincerely believe what they demonstrate for. Their efforts to prevent nuclear war are commendable. It is also true that what they do is brought about in a substantial manner by the activities of the Kremlin through the agency of the KGB. At the start of the movement the Soviet Union enthusiastically supported it because it would have locked them into a position of military superiority at a time when the United States was far behind the Soviets and had started to do something to secure parity for the defense of Europe and the United States.

John Barron's article "The KGB's Magical War for 'Peace' " introduced an overwhelming array of evidence to show that the KGB was the originator and proponent of many of the protest movements favoring an immediate nuclear freeze. Typical of KGB efforts was the case of Vadim Leonov, a Tass correspondent who kept in close contact with Dutch peace leaders. Under the influence of alcohol he made a statement to a Dutch counterintelligence source which resulted in his being expelled from the country. He boasted:

> If Moscow decides that 50,000 demonstrators must take to the streets in the Netherlands, then they take to the streets. Do you know how you can get 50,000 demonstrators at a certain place within a week? A message through my channels is sufficient.[1]

The KGB has constantly employed what they call active measures to convince people around the world that America is for war, whereas the Soviet Union is for peace. They always claim that anything America does endangers the peace of the world; what the Soviets do promotes and furthers peace. What peace means to them is not what peace means to the West. For them it is the absence of opposition to communism. Whoever does anything which is not in accord with the Communist program is a warmonger. One of the Soviets most useful agencies is the World Peace Council, an organization formed in 1950 in France. It was expelled from that country in 1951 for subversion. The headquarters were relocated in Prague and then moved on to Vienna in 1954. In 1957 the Austrian Government sent it packing because of its subversive activities. It now works out of Helsinki with no likelihood whatever of being evicted so long as Finland is under the thumb of the Soviet Union. At no time has the World Peace Council criticized any Soviet acts. It has always orchestrated its public statements in the interests of the Soviets. Romesh Chandra, the president of the council, was quoted as saying, "The World Peace Council in its turn positively reacts to all Soviet initiatives in international affairs." It went so far as to endorse the Soviet Union's invasion of Afghanistan.

Spreading Propaganda

One of the important reasons for the Soviets' campaign for a nuclear freeze arose out of the development of the enhanced-radiation warhead (ERW) by the United States. At the time of the announcement to go ahead with the new device, the Soviets reacted negatively. It would make tens of thousands of Soviet tanks vulnerable, and from a strategic viewpoint virtually useless. The Soviets warned the Europeans that the use of the neutron bomb, as it was inaccurately labeled, would be catastrophic; it would threaten all mankind with extinction. Tass asked the question, directed to Jimmy Carter, "How can one pose as a champion of human rights and at the same time brandish the neutron bomb, which threatens the lives of millions of people?" The Soviets were saying that the neutron bomb would save the United States but destroy Europe. At that time West Germany was surrounded by 20,000 Soviet tanks. The new device was designed as a defensive weapon to prevent the Soviets from taking over West Germany. Was the neutron bomb all the Soviets claimed it to be?

The ERW (neutron bomb) was quite different. It could be fired from a howitzer or a short-range missile. It would obliterate the enemy within a limited radius. Neutrons would be released which would penetrate any tank as easily as light goes through a window. Any human beings within that small area would be killed. One way or another, life within a radius of one mile would be destroyed. The effects of the warhead radiation was short-term. Within a few hours anyone could safely enter the area where the warhead had exploded. By its use, whole divisions of enemy armaments and troops would be wiped out, but few, if any, civilians would be hurt if they were out of the battle area. Physical consequences would be minimal. Europe could be defended against the Communists, leaving most of the people, factories, and other buildings intact. It was essentially a defensive weapon to be used only *after* the enemy had inaugurated an attack on a non-Communist European power. It was a retaliatory device, not an offensive weapon. This weapon was not comparable to the bombs used on Hiroshima or Nagasaki, which resulted in longer-range danger to life and property.

During the period when the neutron bomb was being discussed, and as the intense propaganda campaign was circling the globe, the *New York Times,* by no means a right-wing advocate of nuclear escalation in international affairs, commented:

> Ever since the Carter Administration asked the Congress last summer for funds to produce the enhanced-radiation nuclear warheads, critics ranging from the Soviet propagandists to Western cartoonists have had a field day at the so-called "neutron bomb." The archetypical capitalist weapon, Moscow has called it, a destroyer of people but not property. Grim forecasts of lingering radiation deaths have filled newspaper columns worldwide. Rarely have the relevant questions been asked: Is the neutron weapon really more terrible than other nuclear weapons? And more important, would its employment make nuclear war more likely? The answer to both these questions is almost certainly 'No' . . . Neutron weapons in Western hands would significantly complicate Soviet tactical planning: If its tanks were to attack in mass, they would be highly vulnerable. If they were to disperse they would be easier targets for conventional precision-guided anti-tank weapons. . . .[2]

As a result of the propaganda efforts of the Soviets, the Carter administration canceled the development of the ERW. The Communists rejoiced in what they called the most successful political campaign since World War II. When the ERW effort was terminated, the United States was not accorded a single compensatory concession from the Soviets. The Europeans were not reassured, for the Soviets were setting up their SS-20 missiles which could in a fifteen-minute period obliterate almost a thousand European targets, including virtually all sizable cities in that region. Ben Haden, an evangelical radio and television broadcaster, had this to say: "I can't be a true American and simultaneously an apologist for the Soviet Union. It amazes me that over 250 new nuclear missiles were put in Europe by the Soviets . . . and there wasn't a single protest; only when there's response from the Americans."[3]

The neutron bomb effort was halted, but it didn't stop the Soviets. They went about installing the chillingly effective and destructive SS-20 missiles without a murmur and without any significant demonstrations around the world. When the Reagan administration sought to redress the imbalance, the furor started.

Answering the Protestors?
Prime Minister Pierre Elliot Trudeau of Canada wrote an open letter to those who protested the installation of cruise missiles in Europe by the United States. He had received many letters.

> My purpose is to explain the position of the Government of Canada on the testing of the cruise missile and the broader issue of disarmament. . . .
>
> In recent years, the Soviet Union has deployed hundreds of new SS-20 missiles, each equipped with three nuclear warheads, capable of reaching all the great cities of Europe. However, there has not been any significant outburst of public opposition, either inside or outside the USSR.
>
> That the Soviet people have not protested this action of their leaders surprises no one. What is surprising, however, is that those in the West who are opposed to new nuclear weapons have remained relatively silent about the installation of the SS-20s. In contrast, they are now taking to the streets

to oppose the possible deployment of American Pershing II and cruise missiles to protect Europe against the Soviet nuclear threat.

What is particularly suprising in Canada is to see protesters opposing the possible testing of cruise missiles in Canadian territory, but not opposing the fact that similar missiles are already being tested in the Soviet Union as was confirmed in December by General-Secretary Andropov.

Because people in the free world feel powerless to influence the leaders of the USSR, there is a great temptation to direct the whole force of their anguish and their protests against the only decision-makers who are sensitive to public opinion, namely the leaders of the democratic countries.

Having convinced themselves that it is useless to denounce the SS-20s, people find it easier, I suppose, to forget about them. The strange result of this forgetfulness is that it somehow becomes possible to portray the Soviet Union not as the aggressor, but as the innocent target. This represents a curious amnesia and reversal of roles, which the Soviet leaders are quick to exploit for their own purposes. . . .

I believe that the Soviet people desire peace just as much as the people of the free world. But I also know that the Soviets are very heavily armed. In these circumstances, it would be almost suicidal for the West to adopt a policy of unilateral disarmament, or a policy of suffocating the development of new means of defending ourselves against the Soviet SS-20s. That is the kind of heroic moral choice which an individual could make in his own personal life, but does anyone have the right to impose that choice upon a whole nation, or upon the community of free countries?

When the choice is between steadfastness or weakness in the face of totalitarianism history should have taught us that to refuse to risk one's life in defence of liberty is to risk losing liberty, without any guarantee of saving one's life.[4]

Prime Minister Trudeau is not a theologian; yet his letter reflects ethics within the Judeo-Christian tradition. He recognized the evil of the Soviets and their aggressions. He knew that Soviet propaganda was designed to make the West look immoral and the USSR angelic. He argued that moral choice required the West to defend itself against Soviet aggression. And while he carefully defended the right of an individual to choose a pacifist or unilateral disarmament stance, he questioned the moral right of such people to impose that choice upon Canada or the nations of the world. Thus Trudeau was saying that the issue is deeper than that of simple prudence or strategic necessity alone. It is a choice which must be based on moral considerations.

Noting Military Imbalance

In March of 1983 Secretary of Defense Caspar W. Weinberger issued the second edition of *Soviet Military Power*. He presented a chart showing the force comparison between NATO and the Warsaw Pact parties in Europe in late 1981 (see Figure 9.1). It shows very clearly the great imbalance in the armaments of NATO and those of the Warsaw Pact countries. What many observers may fail to note is one brutal fact of history having to do with the balance of power concept. Whenever opposing nations align themselves by treaties or pacts with a relatively equal balance of power, the likelihood of war is measurably lessened. When one side has a superiority of power, the likelihood of war is greatly increased. This pattern has been demonstrated in the history of Europe. The beginning of World War II came about precisely because the Fascist powers enjoyed military superiority and were willing to use it in the European theatre. The only reason for the defeat of the German-Italian-Japanese axis was the entrance of the United States into the war. Had the United States refrained from entering the war, the Axis powers would have been victorious. Secretary Weinberger made the military imbalance clear in his report.

In the early eighties the Soviets wanted an immediate nuclear freeze, to continue their military position of superiority and to prevent the United States from achieving a balance of power and so prevent war. The advantage lay with the Soviets, and that advantage has been growing. It can be expected to grow even more, so that the situation would become more disparate in another few years.

NATO-WARSAW PACT Force Comparison (in place in Europe—1981)

Figure 9.1

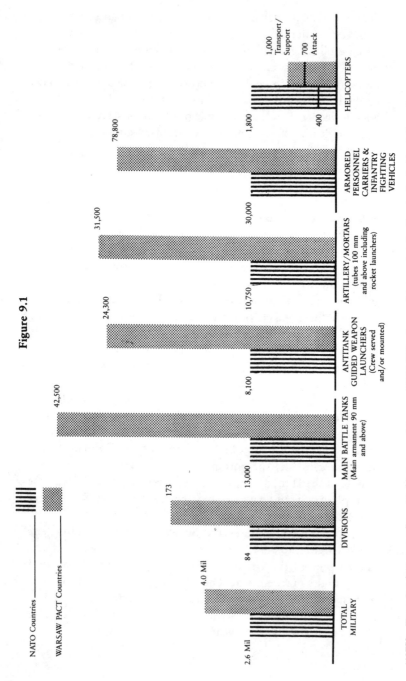

NATO Countries ▬▬▬
WARSAW PACT Countries ▒▒▒

NOTES: Warsaw Pact divisions normally consist of fewer personnel than many NATO divisions but contain more tanks and artillery, thereby obtaining similar combat power.

Forces in place in NATO Europe. Warsaw Pact Forces as far east as but excluding the three western military districts in western Russia (Moscow, Volga and Ural Military Districts).

Dealing in Illusion

Joseph D. Lehman was the principal spokesman at the opening of the intermediate-range nuclear force talks in Geneva in 1981, and at the Strategic Arms Reduction Talks in Geneva in 1982. In an abstract of an article he wrote for *The Annals of the American Academy of Political and Social Science* he said:

> The advent of the Reagan Administration brought about a radically new approach to the issue of nuclear arms control. Some have said that this new approach is really going to destroy the process altogether, while others believe it to be a more realistic and thus more promising opportunity for real arms reduction. One of the negative reactions has been the rise of the nuclear freeze movement. The constituent groups of this movement are diverse but share a common trait: they depend on, or deal in, illusion. For that is what arms control was under SALT, and is under the freeze. These groups are a large number of more or less sophisticated but genuinely concerned and fearful citizens; a group of opportunistic politicians; and the arms control community-in-exile. Unless and until these groups recognize the failures of the past and the necessity of abandoning self-delusion, we will inevitably repeat our mistakes, and arms control will again put form before substance.[5]

The author does not pretend to speak for the U.S. government in this abstract or the article itself. The unfortunate fact is that the media in large measure are skeptical of anything the government says. This skepticism has now reached a point where the American public is becoming more and more skeptical of the media. This has been brought about by the willingness of the media to believe almost anything the Soviets say and to give them the benefit of the doubt under the most damning circumstances. But when it comes to the United States and its activities in matters dealing with Cuba, El Salvador, Nicaragua, or Grenada, the media often take the side of the Soviets. They assume guilt on the part of the United States and innocence on the part of the revolutionaries and aggressors. That media influence has found its way into the largest collegiate institutions in the land, was obvious when Jeane Kirkpatrick, American ambassador to the United Nations, was unable to speak at the University of California at Berkeley.

Roger H. Prior, a student at Harvard University, wrote to the editor of the *National Review*:

> It was refreshing to see reported, in your October 28 (1983) issue, how shabbily Jerry Falwell was treated when he tried to speak at our school, Harvard. An even more serious incident occurred on November 17, when Secretary of Defense Caspar Weinberger, a Harvard graduate, tried to speak at his alma mater. I emphasize the word "tried." Red dye, water balloons, and vulgarities were hurled at the Secretary by the Cambridge elite. Under such hostile circumstances, one would expect the speech to be cancelled, but this was not the case. Ignoring a group of students who attempted to rush the podium, Weinberger kept his cool and finished his speech. Although some of us students who wanted to hear the Secretary's speech were prevented from doing so, we were treated to a rare display of mindless animalistic behavior not witnessed generally, I'm sure, outside of zoological laboratories.[6]

Postponing the Freeze

Given all of the ambiguities, the propagation of false views, and the difficulties inherent in a nuclear freeze, what should be the attitude of Christians who would like to see significant arms reductions and the end of all nuclear weaponry? Why not a nuclear freeze immediately? Is this not a good place to start? With the evidence we now have, an immediate nuclear freeze appears undesirable for the following reasons.

It would lock the West into an inferior military position *vis-a-vis* the Soviets. Europe would be unable to defend itself against aggression, and the United States would be at a great disadvantage militarily. The West would keep the terms of the immediate freeze, but the Soviets would continue to expand their capacity, even as they consistently violated the Salt I and Salt II agreements and other treaties.

Since the Soviets have never agreed to open inspection to guarantee that there is no cheating on their treaties, we have no reason to suppose they will ever agree to such a procedure.

A nuclear freeze at this time would ensure the continued undermining of non-Communist governments. The Soviets' announced intention to bring about the final collapse and destruction of capitalism would be enhanced. Anyone who thinks this is not true of the Soviets is badly misinformed or naive. Whatever name is given to the relationship between the Soviets and the free world—détente, peaceful cooperation, nuclear freeze, or cold war—it is a war being fought at all levels and under differing circumstances around the world.

Whoever in the West wants an immediate nuclear freeze is willing to guarantee to the Soviets a superiority which will enable them to do as they please. It would be tantamount to surrender and would lead to complete subjugation by the Communists. Peace would come, but it would be a peace similar to that in the Soviet Union itself, in Cambodia, in Cuba, and in Mainland China where freedom is dead. Does this mean the West should not work for a nuclear freeze? Not at all! But before such an agreement can be put in place, certain conditions must be met.

First, a balance of power must be established between the West and the Soviets which would make it unlikely and undesirable for either side to start a nuclear war. This means there must be relative military stability in which neither side has a striking power disproportionate to the other. Second, open inspection must be guaranteed to ensure neither side is cheating on its commitment to cease further laboratory work for the development of new and more lethal weaponry. Open inspection would also ensure that no additional nuclear weapons would be added to the stockpile subsequent to the signing of the freeze agreement. Third, the agreement would have to include land and ocean armaments, to rule out addition of nuclear-equipped submarines after the agreement went into effect. Fourth, the agreement would have to include no replacement of nuclear weapons for reasons of age.

Nobody knows if this is possible, but efforts should be made to bring it about. While the endeavors proceed, the West is left with a single alternative to make it unlikely that the Soviets will use their nuclear devices. That alternative is nuclear deterrence.

11

Nuclear Deterrence

Of the possible alternatives at this time, nuclear deterrence is the only viable option in the quest for nuclear disarmament. One compelling reason is that we cannot trust the Soviets. Past and present history affirms that this is so. There have been changes in tactics, advancement in theory, and the talk of peace, détente, and defusing the bomb, but there has been no change in the basic objectives of communism. Unceasingly the Soviets and their compatriots have trumpeted the same line— the death of "imperialism" (capitalism) and the final victory of the proletariat over the bourgeoisie. As a result, we trust and distrust the Marxists. We trust them to do that to which they are committed, but we can't trust them to keep agreements; we can't trust their actions. They lie, cheat, and steal with impunity. They have broken treaties; they have falsified documents and used them for purposes of misinformation. For the Soviets, the end justifies the means, so that when they give their word they do it with the intention of keeping it as long as it advances their cause. They will reverse any agreement when they think it will help them more than keeping their word.

Another reason we must choose nuclear deterrence is the record of the Soviets as troublemakers who stoop to anything to create friction and overthrow non-Marxist regimes. Past and current activities in Africa, in Latin America, in the Far East, particularly in Korea, tell the same story. The Middle East is also within the arena for active Marxist penetration and possible takeovers. Afghanistan, Poland, Czechoslovakia, Latvia, and Hungary stand as monuments to Soviet oppression where man is dehumanized and freedom abolished with little hope of its recovery unless it is secured by another kind of revolution.

No other nation on the earth has the same sort of record for espionage as the Soviets. Hardly a nation exists that has not had to expel Soviet agents and spies who have infiltrated government. The KGB, whose members constitute perhaps the largest body of spies ever assembled by any nation any time, are virtually omnipresent in their far-flung activities. They tap the secret councils of the West, buy information from men of cupidity who violate the first principle of love for their countries and who secretly become Communists, and undermine democracy wherever it exists.

The current upsurge of terrorism springs from Marxist activities in which traitors are trained under Communist leadership to kill, maim, and create fear so as to make a Marxist takeover easier. The Marxists dream up, support, and carry out large demonstrations around the world, though no one in Communist countries can demonstrate against Marxism. Since the Marxists have no concern for their own people, who could suppose that they would have any greater concern for people in the West who believe in democracy and practice free enterprise?

Communist Advance
The Marxists have set up Cuba as the staging-ground for Communist advance in the Americas. They pour hundreds of millions of dollars into this crusade to communize the Americas and to bring the United States to its knees. Their success has been phenomonal, and the future is fraught with perils. The Marxists forever insist that the problems of Central and Latin America are caused by the United States and its "imperialism." They have said it often enough that substantial numbers of Americans have come to accept the charge as though it were true. All of this should convince even the skeptics that the choices of the West are limited, that the only way Marxism can be held at bay is by employing a nuclear shield which will

prevent the Soviets from starting a nuclear war because it would be so costly for them.

No indictment against permitting the Marxists to maintain a disproportionate balance of power can equal that of Alexander Solzhenitsyn, who warns us from experience.

> Communism is unregenerate; it will always present a mortal danger to mankind. It is like an infection in the world's organism: it may lie dormant, but it will inevitably attack with a crippling disease. There is no help to be found in the illusion that certain countries possess an immunity to communism: any country that is free today can be reduced to prostration and complete submission. . . .
>
> Communism is inimical and destructive of *every* national entity. . . . Try asking a malignant tumor what makes it grow. It simply cannot behave otherwise. The same is true of communism; driven by a malevolent and irrational instinct for world domination, it cannot help seizing even more lands. Communism is something new, unprecedented in world history; it is fruitless to seek analogies. . . .
>
> Communism stops only when it encounters a wall, even if it is only a wall of resolve. The West cannot now avoid erecting such a wall in what is already its hour of extremity. Meanwhile, however, twenty possible allies have fallen to communism since World War II. Meanwhile, Western technology has helped develop the terrifying military power of the Communist world. The wall will have to be erected with what strength remains. The present generation of Westerners will have to make a stand on the road upon which its predecessors have so thoughtlessly retreated for sixty years.
>
> But there is hope. All oppressed peoples are on the side of the West: the Russians, the various nationalities of the U.S.S.R., the Chinese and the Cubans. Only by relying on *this* alliance can the West's strategy succeed. Only together with the oppressed will the West constitute the decisive force on earth. This is also a matter of principle, if the West is to uphold freedom everywhere and not merely for itself.
>
> This strategy will obviously entail radical conceptual

changes and the rethinking of tactics on the part of Western politicians, diplomats and military men.

Five years ago, all my warnings were ignored by official America. Your leaders are free to ignore my present predictions as well. But they too will come true.[1]

Anyone who takes Solzhenitsyn seriously, and I do, must realize that the only choice left to the West is the establishment of a nuclear shield of such a level that there will be a balance of power. Only this will convince the Marxists that they cannot use nuclear weaponry without the gravest threat to themselves. Mutual Assured Destruction (MAD), bad as it sounds, is for the present the best instrument of containment to keep the Soviets from employing nuclear weapons to defeat the "imperialists."

Hard Questions to Answer

Once we make a commitment to nuclear deterrence, there are still tough problems to deal with. One is the possibility that even worse instruments of destruction will be developed. We know from scientific advances of the last fifty years that humankind has only begun to tap the secrets of nature. What we do not know is infinitely greater than what we do know. We can therefore expect that more frightening discoveries will test the sanity of men and of nations. This is a reality no one can stop if for no other reason than that science itself does not know what will come out of the quest for knowledge. Moreover, the mind of man is so constituted that it will never be satisfied to let things stay as they are. Cloning, genetic control, and other advances in biology, for example, illustrate the pursuit of knowledge despite the fact that no one can be sure what people of the next generation will do with the new knowledge. Every advance has potential in it for good or for evil. Since all men are not good, the possibility of their capitulation to evil and the wrong use of additional knowledge for wicked purposes is always with us and will be until the end of time.

When we speak of nuclear deterrence, we must do so in the context of the possibility of further developments and ask the question whether the pursuit of more deadly weaponry will continue *ad infinitum.* Surely wisdom would suggest that once the balance of power has been established to a point of relative equality there would be no need for further development of nuclear weapons. This depends on the willingness of the Soviets and the West to accept such a state, and a guarantee that neither would violate the terms of an agreement. It means that both sides would have first-strike capability. We have no reason to suppose that the West would not be satisfied with such a balance of power, but we do have reason to think the Soviets might not be satisfied and that they would violate an agreement as they have others in the past. What purpose would be served for either side to continue to develop more weaponry unless it intended to use it one way or another to eliminate the "enemy"? A system of inspection would be necessary to detect violations by either side. The West has always opted for open inspection; the Soviets have always refused the offer. Will the Soviets change that stand in the interest of a balance of power and peace?

Apart from the question of a bilateral inspection agreement and a decision to stop further production of nuclear devices, there are two other problems. One has to do with the efforts of the West to catch up with the Soviets in order to establish a balance of power. At the heart of this pursuit is the issue of first-strike capability. No balance of power can exist if one side does not have first-strike capability, though the existence of this capability does not mean it will be used. If the Soviets have first-strike capability and the West does not, the Soviets have the upper hand. They would not then need to use that first-strike capability except as a club or as a terroristic agency to bring about the defeat of the West. If only the Soviets enjoyed first-strike capability, the West might reasonably decide against any nuclear shield and resort to unilateral disarmament or pacifism, or a freeze which would produce the same result. If it is ethically or morally wrong for the West to have a first-strike capability, why would it be right for the Soviets to have it?

Some who oppose nuclear weaponry have suggested that

if a nuclear shield is created, the West should adopt the policy that it will not use this weaponry or at least that it will promise there will be no first-strike by the West. Either of these recommendations would leave the West powerless. The Soviets could then proceed to carry out their warfare in every nonnuclear area without fear of reprisal. The West, if it works for parity with the Soviets, should avoid a promise that it will not use nuclear weaponry or that it would never use its first-strike capability.

The second problem having to do with any further development of armed might relates to a present undeniable fact; nuclear war could break out at any time given the number of nuclear weapons available to both sides. If this is true, then it becomes clear that a policy of nuclear deterrence in and of itself is hardly the answer to the present dilemma. Nuclear deterrence would be only an immediate necessity and must be accompanied by the most serious efforts to bring about a nuclear freeze as the starting-point for further efforts to rid the world of nuclear and conventional armaments.

Enough nuclear weapons are in existence right now to do great damage. In one sense, therefore, additional weaponry would not change the basic situation. If it is true that the world powers have enough nuclear weapons to destroy civilization as we now know it, the additional weapons that might be developed would not change the picture materially.

In all of the discussions about nuclear holocaust the words coolness, reason, prudence, intelligence, and goodwill are mentioned. Unfortunately these virtues are in small supply. Hatred, madness, anger, bitterness, and irrationality abound in the hearts of men everywhere. The simplest understanding of original sin should convince the most innocent that we live in a world beset by evil as well as good. If all men were good, there would be no need for a policy of nuclear deterrence. Nor would there be aggression and oppression. The bottom line of the current impasse is that there are evil people, and they are not apt to change. Peace in our time is a vain hope apart from divine intervention, which will come with the Second Advent of Jesus Christ, the Prince of Peace. From the Christian perspective it is not the path of wisdom to capitulate to evil, but to fight against it. A policy of nuclear deterrence is in keeping with that viewpoint.

How Much Deterrence?

How much weaponry the West needs to assure deterrence is difficult to say. Most of us who do not have access to all the facts cannot answer this. New techniques can make forms of weaponry absolete. We do know that the neutron bomb brings ill tidings to the Soviets and their tens of thousands of tanks that surround the European democracies. This nuclear theatre weapon which has short-lived and minor radiation effects is currently the surest guarantee against tank warfare. Weapons that can destroy airborne nuclear devices *before* they land provide security and offer a haven from that form of threat. Individual citizens have every right to speak their piece, but the final decisions on weaponry must be made by those who have been given the responsibility for doing so by the democratic processes. That is why we have a defense department, a president, and a congress. If we don't like their decisions, we can turn them out of office and replace them with others.

In the United States, advocates from every perspective present their cases through the media. Some of the most vocal are not representative of the majority and create an atmosphere of dissent that encourages the Communists to use this dissent as a tool to press their own case. Dissent constitutes both a strength and a weakness for the democracies. If the West must destroy its own freedom in order to meet the Communist threat, then that price would be too high. Yet it is a risk of freedom we must take.

Critics of America's present policy to build a system of deterrence that balances out approximately with that of the Soviets distrust America's leadership. Many are suspicious of America's military personnel. They doubt their intentions, attribute to them a desire for war, and accuse them of overestimating the real military needs of the nation. Many in the upper echelons of our military establishment are men of high integrity who have earned the trust of the nation over a long period of time. This does not mean there are not those who spend more money than necessary or who demand more than what the actual needs are for the defense of the nation. A military leader usually asks for more than he expects to get, hoping that in the end he will get as much as he really thinks the situation calls for. This is not a military problem. It exists in all phases of government, and no programmer is likely to ask only for the amount he really requires for the sustaining of his program.

Is MAD Enough?

The present strategy of the West is based on the acronym MAD—that is, Mutually Assured Destruction. Since both sides can destroy each other, it is assumed that neither side will start a nuclear war. But as we have suggested, there can be a continuing buildup of weaponry, and with additional knowledge even more destructive weapons can come to the fore. Is MAD the final possibility or must we go beyond that? Senator Pete Wilson, from California, spoke to this issue in an interesting and challenging way.

> The President [that is, Mr. Reagan] described (an) exciting prospect this way: "What if free people could live secure in the knowledge that their security did not rest upon the threat of instant U.S. retaliation to deter a Soviet attack; that we could intercept and destroy strategic ballistic missiles before they reached our own soil or that of our allies? Would it not be better to save lives than avenge them?"
>
> "Mutually assured destruction" has stood the test of time, but that does not lessen our anxiety about the continued nuclear build-ups required to assure adequate deterrence. Instead of accepting MAD, we must develop alternatives to it. Instead of finding newer ways to walk the nuclear treadmill, we must get off the treadmill altogether.
>
> Thanks to our space program, there are merging technologies that could work in tandem to destroy an enemy's weapons before they reach targets in the United States. . . . Acting together, these technologies would form layers of defense aimed at running an enemy attack through succes-

sive defensive filters, deep in space and in the ground. Each succeeding filter would winnow offensive weapons before they could detonate on American soil. . . .

The present nuclear arrangement is a treadmill to Armageddon. I don't accept that we must walk that treadmill, numbed to the quest for alternatives, and cowed by fear of the unknown. We find ourselves at one of those moments in history when those with vision and daring can make a real change for the future. To do this, we must articulate a serious, defense-oriented strategy. It won't happen overnight. It won't be a panacea for all our problems, and it probably won't mean the end of all nuclear weapons. Nor will it be easy. Old ideas die hard: Military planners, defense analysts, and government officials have come to understand and accept offense-oriented deterrence. They have grown comfortable—perhaps too comfortable—with it.

As the Italian historian Francesco Guicciardini wrote almost 500 years ago, "You are only truly safe from the man you suspect when he cannot harm you even if he wants to. Security founded on the will and discretion of another is false." This is as true today as it was in the 16th century. We have the opportunity to build a future where our security is based on American know-how rather than on our hopes for rationality and morality in the Soviet leadership.

If we fumble this opportunity, we will continue to live in fear of the day when by accident or design, a nuclear war begins—and we suddenly know that all of our options have finally run out.[2]

Senator Wilson is correct. Nuclear deterrence or MAD is presently the only option, but it is not the end of the matter. All we need to do here is point out that the Senator has omitted a factor in the situation which has had in the past decided influence and powerful effects in the history of the West and of the United States in particular. I refer to the sovereign God in our history. The founding fathers and many presidents since then have called for days of fasting and prayer to the end that God would intervene in the affairs of the nation and provide help in the solution of its problems. Those prayers have not gone unanswered. The blessing of the Almighty has accompanied this nation, but of late the secular spirit has dimmed that truth, and men are leaning on their own devices at a time when, as never before, we need the help of a transcendent God. There is a sense in which America is currently living on the bank account of its ancestors. The day of reckoning may be at hand if this continues and the account is exhausted.

For the West to trust only in nuclear deterrence without also looking to God would be a great mistake. God and the Israelites together won the victory. Moses performed the spiritual rites and the soldiers the physical ones. In 2 Chronicles 20 we read that it was God alone who won the victory for Israel. In both instances, however, God was the important factor in the victories.

Applying Moral Principles to Politics

Some commentators today do not believe that moral principles should be applied to ultimate political questions. Sidney Hook, a philosopher of Jewish descent, argues that morality *is* involved in politics.

The notion that it is better to be a dead lion is woefully inadequate.

> To defend oneself, one must also be ready to die. Men who have the moral courage to fight intelligently for freedom, and are prepared to die for it, have the best prospects of avoiding the fate both of live jackals and of dead lions. Survival is not the be-all and the end-all of a life worthy of man. Sometimes the worst thing that we can know about a man is that he has survived.
>
> Those who say that life is worth living at any cost have already written for themselves an epitaph of infamy, for there is no cause and no person that they will not betray to stay alive. Man's vocation should be the use of the arts of intelligence in behalf of human freedom.[3]

Professor Hook did not speak as a Christian or as an orthodox Jew. He spoke as a man whose presuppositions are carryovers from the Judeo-Christian tradition, a part of the bank account laid up by former generations and not totally used up. Solzhenitsyn, on the other hand, with whom he chose to identify in some measure, was speaking from the vantage point of Christian convictions forged in the gulags of the Soviet Union, where he had suffered until there was holy fire in his heart and a godly determination to eradicate the evil of communism from the face of the globe.

The West has no other choice for the time being than nuclear deterrence, but it is not enough in itself.

12

Facing the Future

As we face the threat of nuclear holocaust, we have to deal with the accompanying fear and hopelessness that is settling over the world. Armageddon is a term we hear to describe what is feared. Everywhere we can detect what might be called the Armageddon spectre. Such a reaction, while understandable in a world in which the secular spirit is dominant, is not based on the biblical Armageddon which will end history and begin a new age ruled by Jesus Christ. When this event takes place, Christ will conquer evil and the age of righteousness and peace will begin. In the current Armageddon syndrome, people do not consider God a participant and no golden age is expected. A depressive hopelessness pervades. When hope evaporates, fear and panic take over, and people cease to function effectively. It is important to work for a recovery of sanity in times that try the soul. A first step is to accept the fact that the road ahead is difficult. Then we must sort out the facts from the myths.

In an article Edward Teller, father of the H-bomb, lists myths about the bomb.[1] One is that the ozone layer would be destroyed and all life would die. While it is true that a holocaust could be expected, all life would not perish. Another myth is that radioactive fallout would make life on the planet uninhabitable, with all food and water supplies polluted. Even though the number of the dead could be substantial, the duration of the radioactivity is relatively short and recovery would be certain. Life would go on.

In the case of Hiroshima and Nagasaki, ordinary bomb shelters were virtually undamaged, even when buildings were leveled. Frame houses that were well-constructed and lying a mile from the center of the bomb blast in Hiroshima were not destroyed. Ninety-eight percent of the people 1.6 to 3.1 miles removed from ground zero survived. Genetic damage to survivors has been relatively minimal. The incidence of cancer among survivors was greater than normal, but did not increase alarmingly. Without minimizing actual damage, it can be said that frightened people have exaggerated the situation. This is part of the Armageddon syndrome.

Another myth associated with the nuclear problem is that further experimentation and development of nuclear weaponry is bound to make the situation worse. Dr. Teller has shown that the opposite is true. Bombs are cleaner. The neutron bomb is useful for battle purposes and has a limited impact on civilian populations. If the West can produce a nuclear shield that will destroy missiles in the air, the ground will not be affected and damaged to the atmosphere would be slight. Dr. Teller's appraisal indicates that the current sense of despair can be dissipated by understanding the facts. When fear is displaced by knowledge and by a sense of hope, men can grapple with difficulties and prepare for contingencies with courage and expectancy.

More emphasis should be placed on the idea that we don't need to give in to communism or to die in a holocuast. Nuclear deterrence has kept the world from nuclear engagement for a long period of time, and when effective defensive systems are made operational, the nuclear threat will be lessened considerably. The future is not as bleak as some have pictured it. People in the West must understand that the Communists use every device to keep the non-Communist world fraught with anxiety. One way is through the Communist "peace" movements which spread the word that Armageddon is just around the corner. If the balance of power is altered in favor of the Communists, the more their peace proposals will be tied to the fear syndrome.

A Western Manifesto

Propaganda can be good or bad. The Communists have made the most of their bad propaganda. The West should launch an intensive propaganda offensive in which our position *vis-a-vis* Communism is stated plainly and publicly in the form of a Western Manifesto.

In it the West must acknowledge that the world is in the grip of a struggle between two opposing ideologies. Ultimate coexistence is impossible because the Communists teach that capitalism is doomed; thus any period of peaceful coexistence is aimed at strengthening the Communist world before it takes the next step toward annihilating the West. The struggle can be resolved only if (1) the Communist world changes its outlook, forsakes its ideology, and engages the West in friendly competition to see which system most improves the lot of mankind, or if (2) the two systems collapse. We in the West must have confidence in our system; we must proclaim that it will survive communism and that we will do whatever is necessary to defeat communism wherever it exists. The West must make it clear that there will be no capitulation to communism and that every advance will be met by resistance. In other words, if the Communists are to win the day, they must do it by force; but the cost to them will be so prohibitive that they will not risk the extermination of their own system.

The West must say flatly that the balance of power will be retained and strengthened by NATO against the Warsaw Pact. Any threat to one member is a threat to all. Any force used against another member is force against all of NATO. The United States must be committed to NATO and ready to assist any of its partners if and when they come under assault by the Communists. This should not rule out negotiation from a position of strength, but there will be no more Munichs for the West. Some things are not negotiable. Thus the Soviet insistence that the Pershing missiles first be withdrawn from Europe before they will discuss arms limitation again is nonnegotiable. The missiles must stay until the Soviets are ready to talk and never be removed unless the Soviets do what is necessary to make removal safe for the West.

We in the West must proclaim our commitment to human rights for all peoples, including those in the Soviet Union, Mainland China, and Cuba, as well as in the captive nations behind the Iron Curtain and in Afghanistan. We should state that we will work unceasingly for the freedom of the captive nations. We should make a distinction between the enslaved peoples under the Communist yoke and the Marxist masters who perpetuate that enslavement. We should communicate this message by radio, television, and the printed word; we must tell the world that whether it takes a year, a decade, or half a century the West will not falter until the enslaved peoples of the world are free.

There should be nonviolent demonstrations for peace throughout the world at every Communist embassy. Marchers with flags, banners, and slogans should sing for the freedom of captive nations. The nations of the West should use the United States as a forum to press the claims for peace and security for all peoples. Friendship for all peoples, including those under dictatorships of the right as well as those under dictatorships from the left, should be high on this agenda.

The peace effort must emphasize the necessity for seeking a nuclear freeze and then go on from that to nuclear disarmament and conventional disarmament. There is little hope that such an effort will succeed so long as the Communist mindset remains unchanged, but the endemic economic difficulties inherent in socialism offer hope. Communism may well fall by the wayside as age overtakes it. Human needs are always subordinated in monolythic systems so that their promises of improving the lot of men are now known to be a mirage. Meanwhile the free nations of the world can demonstrate the usefulness of capitalism to provide men with more of the necessities of life.

Whatever programs come into play among the nations of the West, they will be less than effective unless there is a return to patriotism—particularly in the United States.

A Resurgent Patriotism
In recent years patriotism in the United States has been a casualty of the times. Involvement of the nation in Vietnam, the

activities of the media which often have been antiestablishment and antigovernment, the turning to drugs, as well as selfishness and unrestrained individualism have dimmed the glow of patriotism. The antipatriotic spirit has also suffered due to the activities of historians, including those in the evangelical tradition, who have sought to discount the notion that America is or ever was a Christian nation. Severing God from the American dream and denying the role of Deity in the history of the nation has damaged the fabric of American society and turned it more and more toward secularism. It is time to spread the word that God *is* interested in government and that he plays a determinative role in history.

It may well be true that many in the nation from the beginning of the Republic and now do not have deep religious convictions based on the Judeo-Christian faith; but there have been and are today concerned Christian people whose concern is for the good of the nation. Such groups under God act as a preservative for the nation, for God is pleased to bless smaller numbers and to provide divine aid, especially when the enemy is atheistic and materialistic in its outlook.

In today's climate it might be better to sing the last stanza of "The Star Spangled Banner," which was written by Francis Scott Key in 1814. The nation was at war with the British, the city of Washington and the White House were ravaged by the enemy; but the patriotic spirit was strong, and belief in God was fervent.

> Oh! thus be it ever, when freemen shall stand
>   Between their loved home and the war's desolation!
> Blessed with victory and peace, may the heav'n rescued land
>   Praise the Power that hath made and preserved us
>   a nation.
> Then conquer we must, when our cause it is just,
>   And this be our motto: "In God is our trust."
> And the star-spangled banner in triumph shall wave
>   O'er the land of the free and the home of the brave!

In the two World Wars approximately 15 percent of the number of soldiers under arms were casualties. In the Korean and Vietnam Wars the total casualties were about 3 percent. Most costly was the Civil War with a casualty rate of 32 percent. It was during this war that a somber president, Abraham Lincoln, four months after the battle of Gettysburg, delivered his famous address at the dedication ceremonies. At the end of what was perhaps the shortest, most emotion-packed address any president has given, Abraham Lincoln concluded:

> We were highly resolved that these dead shall not have died in vain—that this nation, under God shall have a new birth of freedom—and that government of the people, by the people, and for the people shall not perish from the earth.

Confidence in God

The same trust and confidence in God expressed by Lincoln are found also in our national hymn, "God of Our Fathers":

> God of our fathers, whose almighty hand
> Leads forth in beauty all the starry band
> Of shining worlds in splendor thru the skies
> Our grateful songs before Thy throne arise.
>
> Thy love divine hath led us in the past,
> In this free land by Thee our lot is cast;
> Be Thou our ruler, guardian, guide, and stay,
> Thy word our law, Thy paths our chosen way.
>
> From war's alarms, from deadly pestilence,
> Be Thy strong arm our ever sure defense;
> Thy true religion in our hearts increase,
> They bounteous goodness nourish us in peace.
>
> Refresh Thy people on their toilsome way,
> Lead us from night to everlasting day;
> Fill all our lives with love and grace divine,
> And glory, laud, and praise be ever Thine![2]

Julia Ward Howe wrote the words to "The Battle Hymn of the Republic," a hymn which is and always will be part of the musical heritage of America. Katherine Lee Bates wrote "America the Beautiful." In all these hymns, the central theme is God and his care over the nation. Edward Everett Hale, clergyman and chaplain to the United States Senate, wrote *A Man Without a Country.* In it he portrayed a nonpatriotic man who was sentenced to exile aboard ship, never to see his native land again. Sir Walter Scott epitomized the meaning of citizenship in one of his poems, the first verse of which says:

Breathes there a man with soul so dead,
Who never to himself hath said,
    This is my own, my native land!
Whose heart hath ne'er within him burned,
As home his footsteps he hath turned,
    From wandering on a foreign strand!
Is such there breathe, go, mark him well;
For him no Minstrel raptures swell;
High though his titles, proud his name;
Boundless his wealth as wish can claim;
Despite those titles, power, and pelf,
The wretch, concentered all in self,
Living shall forfeit fair renown,
And doubly dying, shall go down
To a vile dust from which he sprung
Unwept, unhonored, and unsung.

The lesson America needs to learn anew is that Christianity and patriotism are not contradictory. A follower of the Judeo-Christian tradition should be a patriot. Those who disclaim the impact of Christianity in the founding of the American nation leave unturned innumerable stones beneath which there is evidence to demonstrate that a believing minority clung to God and believed him to be the founding father of the nation.

In a wider context C. S. Lewis dealt with the sentiment of patriotism in his noble book *The Abolition of Man.* He was protesting the stand taken in a school textbook which he felt would lead to the "trousered ape," the "urban blockhead," and "men without chests." He argued that "if nothing is self-evident, nothing can be proved. Similarly, if nothing is obligatory for its own sake, nothing is obligatory at all."[3] "We make men without chests and expect of them virtue and enterprise. We laugh at honour and are shocked to find traitors in our midst. We castrate and bid the geldings be fruitful."[4]

When speaking about patriotism in connection with the defense of one's native land, he mentioned what Johnson had written in a passage from *Western Islands:* "That man is little to be envied, whose patriotism would not gain force upon the plains of Marathon, or whose piety would not grow warmer among the ruins of Iona." He was equally clear when he said:

> When a Roman father told his son that it was a sweet and seemly thing to die for his country, he believed what he said. He was communicating to the son an emotion which he himself shared and which he believed to be in accord with the value which his judgement discerned in noble death. He was giving the boy the best he had, giving of his spirit to humanize him as he had given his body to beget him. But Gaius and Titius [the authors of the book he was criticizing and to which he had given the pseudonym *The Green Book*] cannot believe that in calling such a death sweet and seemly they would be saying 'something important about something.'

C. S. Lewis had fought for his country in World War I. He objected to debunking the notion that to die for the defense of one's country is good. He believed that those who ridicule this noble tradition do what Confucius condemned: "The Master said, He who sets to work on a different stand destroys the whole fabric."[5] Or to quote Lewis's statement from John Bunyan: "It came burning hot into my mind, whatever he said and however he flattered, when he got me to his house, he would sell me for a slave."[6]

Theologians from the earliest days have agreed that it is right for those who stand in the Judeo-Christian tradition to fight and to die for their country when there is a just war to be fought. Who would deny that World War II was a just war, fought against Nazism and Adolf Hitler? How then could it be wrong to fight against the Communists if and when that becomes necessary? They represent that which, when compared on the scale used to judge Hitler, is equal to anything Hitler and his cohorts did.

Calling on God

The coins of America bear the slogan, "In God We Trust." Who would suppose that it is wrong to ask for help from the God the nation professes to trust?

We have advanced the thesis that God is immanent as well as transcendent in the historical processes. He is above history and also in history. He is bringing history to its conclusion in the person of Jesus Christ. If this is true, it should be plain that a sovereign God and his people constitute a majority. We have every reason to be confident that, working together, we will overcome the enemy, whether it be by God alone or God using the resources, gifts, and abilities resident in the nation.

In addition to what is done by the nation, there must be those who call on God for the nation. Prayer is the first resource. Even though God may work silently so that the divine presence is not easily apparent, yet that silent working is essential, and without it there is no hope for overcoming any enemy. Moses, the great lawgiver, said, "For what great nation is there that has a god so near to it as the Lord our God is to us, whenever we call upon him? And what great nation is there, that has statutes and ordinances so righteous as all this law which I set before you this day?" (Deuteronomy 4:7, 8).

God has spoken in the Bible. Let us accept and obey his commandments as expressed in the Ten Commandments. Keeping these is evidence of devotion to the claims of God. Let us claim the promise of God that he will hear and help those who call upon him in faith and in obedience to the divine commandments. Moses also declared that "The secret things belong to the Lord our God; but the things that are revealed belong to us and to our children forever, that we may do all the words of this law" (Deuteronomy 29:29). God gave to his people Israel and to his church today his revelation, which contains all we need for life and survival against every enemy. Some things are hidden from God's people in the secret counsels of the Godhead, but we know that in those secret counsels God does for those who obey his commandments abundantly above all we can ask or even think.

God commands that prayer be made for those in authority over the nation, even those who may not be under the Lordship of God. He causes such people to do his will and to bring about his desires though they know it not. He turns the hearts of kings so that they willingly do what he wants, but they don't realize it. We as a nation must pray, knowing that armaments are not enough, important as they may be. He will provide the power, the skill, and the discernment so that if weapons must be used they will accomplish the right result.

We also must pray for the enemies of the nation, that God will bring them to himself. Beyond that, it is essential to ask God to bring divine judgments on evildoers. He may call some of those leaders from this world to await that final judgment which is to come, or he can prevent them from doing what they seek to accomplish. God can turn the Soviet Union, Cuba, Mainland China, and other Communist nations inside-out overnight, or he can do it over a period of time.

Our churches should be open every day and believing people encouraged to worship and intercede for the nation and its allies. The pastoral prayers of every clergyman should include petitions for the spiritual health of the nation, for the leadership of the nation, and for those who work for the country in even the smallest ways. Let our land tell it abroad that we are seeking the help of the God we profess on our coins, the God who called the nation into being, and the God who will sustain it against the plans of those who want to destroy it.

Let Bible classes around the country unite in prayer for the nation, let small groups meet each week to pray, let individuals spend time on their knees for the country as well as for themselves. When a nation trusts in armaments, it gets what armaments can do; when it trusts in its own wisdom, it gets what human wisdom can do; when it trusts in organization, it gets what organization can do; but when it trusts in God, it gets what God can do. Here the nation can learn the lesson taught by ministers and missionaries in the spiritual realm, knowing that what happens in the spiritual realm as a result of prayer can happen in the temporal realm in the affairs of the nation as well.

Adoniram Judson, the great missionary to Burma, left behind him this statement: "I never was deeply interested in any project, I never prayed sincerely and earnestly for anything, but it came at some time—no matter how distant the day— somehow in some shape, probably the last I should have devised—it came!"[7] Of Pastor Gossner, a German missionary pastor and saint, it was said: "He prayed up the walls of a hospital and the hearts of nurses; he prayed mission stations into being and missionaries into faith; he prayed open the hearts of the rich, and gold from the most distant lands."[8]

Let it be said in the days ahead that God's faithful people in America prayed shut the gulags and the jails of the Communists; that they prayed the end of the enemy's military might, freedom for the shackled victims of Communist aggression, nuclear weaponry out of the world, the deliverance of captives, food to the poor, help to the impoverished, revival to the church of Jesus Christ, and power to the powerless.

Fasting with Prayer
A second and rarely used resource for believers is fasting. It was commended in the Old and New Testaments and practiced in the early church. The purpose of fasting is therapeutic for the practitioners, turns the participant toward spiritual matters for a season, heightens spiritual sensitivity, leads to more prayer, and by the use of the Scriptures results in increased devotion to God. Prayer and fasting go hand in hand. It was effective in American life when many of our presidents called for both fasting and prayer in their public proclamations during times of national crisis. If God was pleased to deliver the nation then, he will be no less pleased to respond to times of fasting and prayer today. When these activities are done in the power of the Holy

Spirit and under the Lordship of Jesus Christ, they have incalculable value.

Hope Here and Now

Third, there is a great need for the recovery of the doctrine of hope. Hopelessness and depression are common ailments today. Thousands of people sit on the couches of psychiatrists and psychologists trying to rid themselves of a disease that is more spiritual than psychological. The Bible speaks of the three graces—faith, hope, and love. Hope, based on the affirmation of Scripture, belongs to believers by right of their rebirth from above. They need not quail before any aggressor, and they need not fear any tyrant. Hope is based upon divine promises, a chief one of which is that God will never leave nor forsake his people. When a nation walks with God, there is hope. When a nation forgets God, hope flees and spiritual depression sets in.

In 1983 Alexander Solzhenitsyn received the Templeton Foundation Award for Progress in Religion. He was cited as a "pioneer in the renaissance of religion in atheist nations . . . a living symbol of the continuing vitality of the Orthodox tradition of spirituality." In his acceptance address Solzhenitsyn said: "The entire twentieth century is being sucked into the vortex of atheism and self-destruction. . . . We can only reach with determination for the warm hand of God, which we have so rashly and self-confidently pushed away. . . . There is nothing else to cling to in the landslide." He warned of the materialism, spiritual vapidity, and timidity of the West in the face of communism. He expressed hope that Americans who believe in God will rejoice in these dark days. He referred to his eight years in the Gulag and the thinking he did there. He said, "I met a great many Orthodox and had a lot of discussions with them. After that, I was mortally ill in camp, and, faced with that mortal illness, I found anew my faith."[9] The bottom line of his address was full of hope and assurance. He said: "No matter how formidably Communism bristles with tanks and rockets, no matter what success it attains in seizing the planet, it is doomed never to vanquish Christianity."[10]

The people of God can face the future with confidence

and hope. Communism is doomed; it shall perish from the earth. Its expectation that the free world shall perish is based on a hope that has no foundation because it leaves God out of the picture. Communism is traveling the Armageddon Road which leads to extinction. Whoever follows that road and sneers at God is bound by the law of self-destruction to fail at last. Those of us who live to fight against this monster should never forget the word that came from the First World War against the Kaiser. The poet spoke for all those who laid down their lives in defense of freedom:

> In Flanders fields the poppies blow
> Between the crosses, row on row,
>> That mark our place; and in the sky
>> The larks, still bravely singing, fly
> Scarce heard among the guns below.
>
> We are the dead. Short days ago
> We lived, felt dawn, saw sunset glow,
>> Loved and were loved, and now we lie
> in Flanders fields.
> Take up our quarrel with the foe:
> To you from falling hands we throw
>> The torch; be yours to hold it high.
> If ye break faith with us who die
> We shall not sleep, though poppies grow
>> In Flanders fields.

That torch we have picked up! That flame we shall keep burning for the generation to come! If we do not succeed in defeating the foe, from falling hands we will throw the torch to those who rise to pick it up to finish communism's march to its Armageddon doom.

Notes

Chapter One: The Nuclear Threat

1. Gordon D. Kaufman, "Nuclear Eschatology and the Study of Religion," *Harvard Divinity Bulletin*, February-March 1983, p. 6.
2. Jonathan Schell, *The New Yorker*, February 8, 1983, pp. 59, 60.
3. Kaufman, "Nuclear Eschatology."
4. *Ibid.*
5. *Ibid.*
6. *Ibid.*

Chapter Four: War in the Old Testament

1. Stephen T. Davis, *The Debate About the Bible* (Philadelphia: Westminster, 1977), pp. 96, 97.
2. William E. May, letter to the editor, *National Review*, May 13, 1983, p. 562.

Chapter Five: The View from the New Testament

1. George A. Buttrick, *The Interpreter's Bible*, Vol. 7 (Nashville: Abingdon, 1951), p. 301.
2. *Ibid.*, p. 373.
3. *Ibid.*, pp. 286, 287.
4. Matthew Henry, *A Commentary on the Whole Bible*, Vol. 5 (Old Tappan, N.J.: Revell, n.d.), p. 52.
5. Jose Miguez-Bonino, *Christians and Marxists: The Mutual Challenge to Revolution* (Grand Rapids, Mich.: Eerdmans, 1976), pp. 7, 8.
6. *Ibid.*, p. 15.
7. *Ibid.*, p. 16.
8. *Ibid.*, p. 88.

9. *Ibid.,* pp. 135, 136.
10. Rene Padilla, "A Reflection on the Just War," *Mennonite Brethren Herald,* November 4, 1983, p. 6.

Chapter Six: The Enemy

1. From *America's Future,* 1983.

Chapter Seven: Communist Principles

1. Gerhart Niemeyer, *Facts on Communism,* Vol. 1, *The Communist Ideology* (Washington D.C.: U.S. Government Printing Office, Committee on Unamerican Activities, 1960), pp. 116ff.
2. *Ibid.,* p. 117.
3. *Samizdat Bulletin,* March 1983, No. 119.
4. Emil Brunner, "And Should Communism Be Victorious?," *Neue Zurcher Zeitung,* May 28, 1961.

Chapter Eight: Pacifism

1. Ronald Sider and Richard K. Taylor, *Nuclear Holocaust and Christian Hope* (Downers Grove, Ill.: InterVarsity Press, 1982), p. 59.
2. *Ibid.,* p. 60.
3. *Ibid.,* p. 12.
4. *Ibid.,* pp. 80, 81.
5. *Ibid.,* p. 120.
6. *Ibid.,* p. 112.
7. *Ibid.,* p. 117.
8. *Ibid.,* p. 274.
9. *Ibid.,* p. 275.
10. *The Register* (Santa Ana, Calif.), December 12, 1983, p. A-7.
11. 1978, Volume 4.
12. These quotations are taken from the booklet *War and Peace: Soviet Russia Speaks,* Albert L. Weeks and William C. Bodie, eds. (New York: National Strategy Information Center, 1983).

Chapter Nine: Unilateral Disarmament

1. Billy Graham, *Approaching Hoofbeats* (Waco, Tex.: Word, 1984), p. 132.
2. John Cardinal Krol, "The Catholic Bishops' Concern with Nuclear Armaments," *The Annals of the American Academy of Political and Social Science,* Vol. 469 (September 1983), pp. 38-45.
3. *Ibid.,* p. 40.
4. *Time,* June 20, 1983, p. 55.

Chapter Ten: Nuclear Freeze

1. John Barron, "The KGB's Magical War for 'Peace,' " *Reader's Digest,* October 1982, p. 232ff.
2. *Ibid.,* p. 229.
3. Ben Haden, "Neutral—So Close, So Far," in *Changed Lives* (Chattanooga: Ben Haden Evangelistic Association, 1983).
4. Pierre Elliott Trudeau, *Reformed Perspective,* Vol. 2, No. 8 (June 1983), p. 10.
5. Joseph D. Lehman, *The Annals of the American Academy of Political and Social Science,* Vol. 469 (September 1983), p. 23.
6. Roger H. Prior, letter to the editor, *National Review,* January 27, 1984, p. 7.

Chapter Eleven: Nuclear Deterrence

1. Alexander Solzhenitsyn, *Time,* February 18, 1980, pp. 48, 49.
2. Pete Wilson, *Los Angeles Times,* March 2, 1984, Part II, p. 11.
3. Sidney Hook, *Los Angeles Times,* May 11, 1983, Part II, p. 13.

Chapter Twelve: Facing the Future

1. Edward Teller, "Dangerous Myths About Nuclear Arms," *Reader's Digest,* November 1982.
2. Daniel C. Roberts, author; George Warren, composer, 1982.
3. C. S. Lewis, *The Abolition of Man* (New York: Macmillan, 1962), p. 53.
4. *Ibid.,* p. 35.
5. Confucius, *Analects,* II, 16.
6. Lewis, *The Abolition of Man,* p. 65.
7. Harold Lindsell, *Missionary Principles and Practice* (Old Tappan, N.J.: Revell, 1955), p. 317ff.
8. *Ibid.*
9. Alexander Solzhenitsyn, *Time,* May 23, 1983, p. 57.
10. *Ibid.*